God's Way to Success

God's Way to Success

JASON GROUBE

God's Way to Success
Published by Jason Groube
with Castle Publishing Ltd
New Zealand

© 2021 Jason Groube
jason.selinagroube@outlook.com

ISBN 978-0-473-58089-6 (Softcover)
ISBN 978-0-473-58090-2 (ePUB)
ISBN 978-0-473-58091-9 (Kindle)

Editing:
Geoff Vause

Production & Typesetting:
Andrew Killick
Castle Publishing Services
www.castlepublishing.co.nz

Cover Design:
Paul Smith

All Scripture quotations, unless otherwise indicated,
are taken from the Holy Bible, New International Version®, NIV®.
Copyright ©1973, 1978, 1984, 2011 by Biblica, Inc.™
Used by permission of Zondervan. All rights reserved worldwide.
www.zondervan.com

Scripture quotations marked (KJV) are taken from
The Authorised (King James) Version.
Reproduced by permission of the Crown's patentee,
Cambridge University Press.

ALL RIGHTS RESERVED

No part of this publication may be reproduced,
stored in a retrieval system, or transmitted
in any form or by any means, electronic, mechanical,
photocopying, recording or otherwise,
without prior written permission from the author.

Contents

Introduction	9
Part One: The Fall of Man	**11**
The Fall	13
Sin and Separation	17
Rebellion	21
The Tree of Knowledge of Good and Evil	25
Part Two: Redemption	**29**
The Passover	31
Repentance	39
Born-again	43
Redemption Prophesied – The Redeemer Foretold	47
The Redemptive Story – From Adam to Noah	61
Isaiah 53	65
Jonah	75
Changing Water to Wine	85
Propitiation	89
Part Three: The Tent of Meeting	**95**
The Tabernacle – The Tent of Meeting	97
To Know God	103
Jesus Christ Our Foundation	109
The Holy Spirit – Connecting Us with God	113

Part Four: Learning the Ways of God — 117

The Spiritual Leviticus Journey — 119
A Duel/Dual to the Death — 127
The Tree of Knowledge Versus the True Vine — 143
Obedience — 151
The Joy of Trials — 157
Afflictions Appointed to Us — 161
Defeating the Giants — 165

Part Five: God's Will for Us — 171

Numbers 1 – Conscripted — 173
Numbers 2-4 – Priestly Duties — 177
Numbers 2 – Placement — 183
Knowing the Good, Pleasing and Perfect Will of God — 187

Conclusion — 191

Real Success

Success can come to any man, woman or child
From amongst the free, the captive, the wild.
No respecter of person, young or old
Visits the beggar and the man of gold.
Knows no borders and takes no side,
Welcomes anyone who puts aside, pride.
The aroma of community he makes sweet
And lights the path of individual feet.
Success will set the captive free,
And gives freedom in captivity.
Success became flesh and walked amongst us
The Messiah, the LORD, the man named Jesus.

Introduction

God's way to success is simple. It simply involves His Son Jesus Christ.

You can achieve great things on this earth, but if you have no relationship with God through Jesus Christ your eternity won't be found. It will be lost. That is hell.

Success has been centred on what we accomplish on this earth. Outward success may accompany many Christians but it's not the fundamental requirement of God. True success can only start when Jesus Christ is the foundation of our lives.

> For no one can lay any foundation other than the one already laid, which is Jesus Christ. If anyone builds on this foundation using gold, silver, costly stones, wood, hay or straw, their work will be shown for what it is, because the Day will bring it to light. It will be revealed with fire, and the fire will test the quality of each person's work. (1 Corinthians 3:11-13)

This scripture is the basis for this book. The foundation must be Christ. Once this foundation is established, we build upon it. If these buildings are of the Lord, they'll survive the fire when we give an account of our lives.

If the buildings are not of the Lord, our works will be burnt up. Success is about knowing Christ and accomplishing what He has for us to do.

> For we are God's handiwork, created in Christ Jesus to do good works, which God prepared in advance for us to do. (Ephesians 2:10)

We are to do what God has called us to do and in submission to Him. We are to be led by the Holy Spirit to know God's will. Walking in the Spirit must increase, while walking in the flesh must decrease.

> Jesus answered, 'Very truly I tell you, no one can enter the kingdom of God unless they are born of water and the Spirit. Flesh gives birth to flesh, but the Spirit gives birth to spirit.' (John 3:5-6)

> Those who live according to the flesh have their minds set on what the flesh desires; but those who live in accordance with the Spirit have their minds set on what the Spirit desires. (Romans 8:5)

How do we accomplish true success? God has given us a pattern for the ability to be successful. You can find this throughout the Bible with a good example found in Genesis through to Numbers. From the beginning of the Bible, we will see a pattern emerge giving solid foundations. From Genesis through to Numbers, there is a progression of five events laying solid foundations for Christians today:

1. (Genesis) The fall of man. Separated from God because of sin.
2. (Exodus) The Passover: The Redeemer and Redemption.
3. (Exodus) The Tent of Meeting: Establishing our relationship with God.
4. (Leviticus) Sacrifices, Clean or Unclean, Lawful or Unlawful: Learning to walk in the Spirit and not the flesh.
5. (Numbers) Placement and duties: God's will for us and accomplishing Christ's good works.

Part 1
The Fall of Man

Chapter 1

The Fall

We will never fully appreciate what happened in the Garden of Eden when Adam ate the forbidden fruit and the effect it has on mankind ever since, and the cost God had to go through to restore it.

But the Bible clearly teaches the problem we find ourselves in, and gives us the solution to get out from under it.

We need to appreciate how deep this cut (the fall of man) actually went.

> But very truly I tell you, it is for your good that I am going away. Unless I go away, the Advocate will not come to you; but if I go, I will send him to you. When he comes, he will prove the world to be wrong about sin and righteousness and judgment; about sin, because people do not believe in me; about righteousness, because I am going to the Father, where you can see me no longer; and about judgment, because the prince of this world now stands condemned. (John 16:7-11)

The only reason Jesus had to come to this earth as a man was because we rebelled against His Word, became alienated from our Creator and unwittingly came under the control of the devil.

The fact God had to send His Son to die a horrendous death

tells us how totally hopeless our situation is. The fall of man found in Genesis clearly tells us this starting point of sin and separation.

> Now the serpent was more crafty than any of the wild animals the LORD God had made. He said to the woman, 'Did God really say, "You must not eat from any tree in the garden"?' The woman said to the serpent, 'We may eat fruit from the trees in the garden, but God did say, "You must not eat fruit from the tree that is in the middle of the garden, and you must not touch it, or you will die."' 'You will not certainly die,' the serpent said to the woman. 'For God knows that when you eat from it your eyes will be opened, and you will be like God, knowing good and evil.' When the woman saw that the fruit of the tree was good for food and pleasing to the eye, and also desirable for gaining wisdom, she took some and ate it. She also gave some to her husband, who was with her, and he ate it. (Genesis 3:1-6)

When Adam and Eve ate the forbidden fruit, sin entered them. We inherited sin. We went from God's kingdom into Satan's. God never created sin, Lucifer did.[1] He is the ultimate personification of sin, and if you take sin to its ultimate pinnacle, to its extreme end, that's Satan.

When sin entered mankind, the devil gained dominion over us. Because the devil hates God, the sin within us hates God.

> Therefore, just as sin entered the world through one man, and death through sin, and in this way death came to all people, because all sinned. (Romans 5:12)

Due to sin, if left to ourselves, we won't pursue our Creator.

---

1   Ezekiel 28:14-15

> God looks down from heaven on all mankind to see if there are any who understand, any who seek God. Everyone has turned away, all have become corrupt; there is no one who does good, not even one. (Psalm 53:2-3)

Again we see in Romans 3:10-12,

> As it is written: 'There is no one righteous, not even one; there is no one who understands; there is no one who seeks God. All have turned away, they have together become worthless; there is no one who does good, not even one.'

One more from John 3:19,

> This is the verdict: Light has come into the world, but people loved darkness instead of light because their deeds were evil.

God has always had to intervene, because when left to ourselves, we have no hope. Jesus made a controversial statement which gives only one answer to this major problem.

> Jesus answered, 'I am the way and the truth and the life. No one comes to the Father except through me.' (John 14:6)

There is only one road taking us out of this sinful trap, not many. If Christ's offer is rejected, anything we do outside of Jesus Christ won't be accepted by God as sufficient access out of the kingdom of darkness and into the kingdom of light.

When Jesus died and rose again, He sent the Holy Spirit to convict the world of sin.

> When he (*Holy Spirit*) comes, he will prove the world to be in

the wrong about sin and righteousness and judgment. (John 16:8)

The Holy Spirit reveals the truth, leading us to repentance through Jesus Christ, breaking us free from the sin of darkness.

> Giving thanks unto the Father, which hath made us meet to be partakers of the inheritance of the saints in light: Who hath delivered us from the power of darkness, and hath translated us into the kingdom of his dear Son. (Colossians 1:12-13 KJV)

From the time of the Garden, sin has been mankind's problem by becoming hopelessly ensnared by its influence and effect.

Only God knew how we could overcome this, giving us the ability to come out of a failed situation and bringing us into His success.

The choice is clear. Failure is a lost eternity. Success is finding eternal life through Jesus Christ and Paradise restored. Failure is continuing to have Paradise lost.

Chapter 2

Sin and Separation

What is sin?

Sin is more than dark evil, or the vices ensnaring us. Sin is anything outside God. Operating independently in our own strength, wisdom and ability without God. Facing triumphs and tribulations without the involvement of God.

Sin is anything we do without God. Literally, to 'miss the mark' or 'be without the Word of God'.

When we ate the fruit from the Tree of Knowledge of good and evil,[2] we became independent from God. We spiritually died and became separated. Sin means we are separated from God and operate without Him.

If we're separated from God here on this earth while we're alive, then we will be separated from God after we die in a much more horrific capacity. A spirit designed to be free, enslaved.

That is why God sent His Son to die on the cross, so we can be reconciled back to Him.

Whoever believes in the Son has eternal life, but whoever rejects

---

2   Therefore, just as sin entered the world through one man, and death through sin, and in this way death came to all people, because all sinned. (Romans 5:12)

the Son will not see life, for God's wrath remains on them. (John 3:36)

The reality of this is too difficult and terrifying to comprehend. We don't fully understand all Jesus came to save us from. What He had to endure through suffering and death should give us a sense of how big this problem was. God desires no one perishes.

> The Lord is not slow in keeping his promise, as some understand slowness. Instead He is patient with you, not wanting anyone to perish, but everyone to come to repentance. (2 Peter 3:9)

Being separated from God is more than facing the fires of hell, which is not the devil's lair.

> Then he will say to those on his left, 'Depart from me, you who are cursed, into the eternal fire prepared for the devil and his angels. (Matthew 25:41)

> And the devil, who deceived them, was thrown into the lake of burning sulphur, where the beast and the false prophet had been thrown. They will be tormented day and night for ever and ever. (Revelation 20:10)

Not even the devil and all his evil minions want to go to hell.

Separation is more than the eternal fires of damnation. It is far worse than that. Man's scriptural imagery cannot adequately describe an eternity in separation.

Think of everything that is good; love, security, well-being, peacefulness, sanity, acceptance, fellowship, friends, hope, purpose, and there is much more which could be added. If you take all that makes this life bearable and then take it all away, you are left with everything that is the opposite of what we want and need. The good which comes from God keeps life on this earth bearable.

> For everything God created is good, and nothing is to be rejected if it is received with thanksgiving. (1 Timothy 4:4)

If you take God out of our existence, you are left with nothing good, but the extreme darkness of suffering, pain, loneliness, hopelessness. No love, no joy, no peace, no sleep, no companionship (those who think they are going to hell to party with their friends are horribly deceived).

There will be many more extremes faced and no end to this in sight, for hell is eternal.

> Then shall he say also unto them on the left hand, Depart from me, ye cursed, into everlasting fire prepared for the devil and his angels. (Matthew 25:41 KJV)

Chapter 3

Rebellion

The fool says in his heart, 'There is no God.' (Psalm 53:1)

If you go back to the original Hebrew sentence, the word 'There' is not in the original verse.[3] The original Hebrew for 'There is no God', reads, '*Ayin Elohim*'. The verse should read, 'The fool says in his heart, "No, God".'

The nature of sin is to rebel against God and mankind is in rebellion. I don't believe the majority of mankind say in their hearts, 'There is no God.' I believe they say, 'No, God.'[4]

This was true for me. When I was 11 years old we were at a Christian conference. I was in the children's meeting when God supernaturally affected me. It was a small encounter, but it was enough to make me realise it was real and I knew He was the Truth and the only Truth. For the next 10 years I said in my heart, 'No, God.'

Even though my knowledge about God is not usual, He does reveal Himself to mankind more than we would like to admit. Whenever God makes us aware of the Lord Jesus Christ, they are supernatural encounters. It gives us the ability to accept or reject.

---

3   *Strong's Hebrew Lexicon* H369 – 'ayin' which means 'no' (not 'there').
4   Romans 1:18-21

The Holy Spirit will reveal the truth, which this world doesn't understand.

> When he comes, he will prove the world to be in the wrong about sin and righteousness and judgment. (John 16:8)

A friend asked me a question bothering him. He asked how a loving God could send people to hell who were not bad people. He was referring to his brother, who he considered, 'a good person who did not deserve to go to hell.'

Not accepting Jesus Christ as Lord was the answer, in as far as any of us can know the answer. I tried to explain why his brother may have rejected this. Before this explanation, we will look at three reasons people reject Christ.

Atheism. There are people who believe once we die, that's it. Some haven't given things much thought and others believe in evolution. Evolution is their god and it justifies their reasoning. It takes more faith to believe evolution as the source of our origins, than to believe in a Creator God. There are some excellent Creation ministries on the internet revealing how stupid evolution is. These are the ones saying, 'There is no God.'

The next reason is self-righteousness. Not the arrogant 'I'm better than thou' one, but the one where our good earns us merits. Most, if not all religions (and human philosophies), outside of Christianity rely on this system.

It's a simple concept. It requires us to perform certain religious duties or some charitable act to win the favour of our deity or to become a better person. Hopefully, our good will earn enough favour to give us a good destiny. If you mix this idea with the teaching many roads lead to heaven, this deception will blind many.

You can't earn your way into heaven no matter how good you are.

> But we are as an unclean thing, and all our righteousnesses are as filthy rags; and we all do fade as a leaf; and our iniquities, like the wind, have taken us away. (Isaiah 64:6 KJV)

The next reason is rebellion. These people say in their heart, 'No, God'. This is what I focused on with my friend.

The Gospel of Jesus Christ has reached many parts of the world and a lot of people have heard about Him. When man finally stands before His Creator, he will be accountable and he will be without excuse.

> The wrath of God is being revealed from heaven against all the godlessness and wickedness of people, who suppress the truth by their wickedness, since what may be known about God is plain to them, because God has made it plain to them. For since the creation of the world God's invisible qualities – his eternal power and divine nature – have been clearly seen, being understood from what has been made, so that people are without excuse. For although they knew God, they neither glorified him as God nor gave thanks to him, but their thinking became futile and their foolish hearts were darkened. Although they claimed to be wise, they became fools. (Romans 1:18-22)

Throughout our lives God will make Himself known to us, and it happens more than we realise. The Bible declares mankind has no excuse, including those who have never heard the Gospel. How God does this I wouldn't have a clue, but the Holy Scripture doesn't lie.

During my teenage years I had no desire to submit to God. But it didn't mean God stopped pursuing me. There were many times when I was aware of God, but in my heart, I said, 'No, God.'

God is not inactive. He will pursue mankind through many ways. It's up to the individual how they respond.

There are many ways they may reject His call. These are some of the responses. 'No, not interested.' 'I don't need Him.' 'He helps the helpless, I'm not helpless.' 'Christianity is too boring.' 'I'm too bad for God.' 'I'm a good person, God knows that.' 'Maybe when I'm older and had my fun.' 'I go to church.' 'I control my destiny.'

This list goes on. One of the reasons mankind finds it hard to surrender to the Lord Jesus is because of rebellion. We willingly rebel against God's promptings and give Him all sorts of excuses why we don't want to respond. Mankind's inclination is to turn their back on God.

> Obey me, and I will be your God and you will be my people. Walk in obedience to all I command you, that it may go well with you. But they did not listen or pay attention; instead, they followed the stubborn inclinations of their evil hearts. They went backward and not forward. (Jeremiah 7:23-24)

The Lord's response to this rebellion is clear and sobering.

> The earth is broken up, the earth is split asunder, the earth is violently shaken. The earth reels like a drunkard, it sways like a hut in the wind; so heavy upon it is the guilt of its rebellion that it falls – never to rise again. In that day the LORD will punish the powers in the heavens above and the kings on the earth below. They will be herded together like prisoners bound in a dungeon; they will be shut up in prison and be punished after many days. (Isaiah 24:19-22)

Chapter 4

The Tree of Knowledge of Good and Evil

The Tree of Knowledge is not a widely discussed subject within Christianity, but it has affected all of us. What makes this tree so destructive is it gave the ability for mankind to go it alone and even believe we too can become gods.

> For God doth know that in the day ye eat thereof, then your eyes shall be opened, and ye shall be as gods, knowing good and evil. (Genesis 3:5 KJV)

The fruit from the Tree of Knowledge brought separation and independence.

The fruit is important, because God judges us by the fruit we produce.

> By their fruit you will recognise them. Do people pick grapes from the thornbushes, or figs from thistles? Likewise, every good tree bears good fruit, but a bad tree bears bad fruit. A good tree cannot bear bad fruit, and a bad tree cannot bear good fruit. Every tree that does not bear good fruit is cut down and thrown into the fire. Thus, by their fruit you will recognise them. (Matthew 7:16-20)

Anyone whose source is only from the Tree of Knowledge will always produce bad fruit.

The only way we can detach ourselves from this tree is to attach ourselves to another – the Tree of Life. The Tree of Life is not a tree, but a person.

> Jesus said, 'I am the way and the truth and the life...' (John 14:6)

We must remember to remain there. God will judge us by the fruit we bear and this is an ongoing process.

> I am the true vine, and my Father is the gardener. He cuts off every branch in me that bears no fruit, while every branch that does bear fruit he prunes so that it will be even more fruitful.
>
> You are already clean because of the word I have spoken to you. Remain in me, as I also remain in you. No branch can bear fruit by itself; it must remain in the vine. Neither can you bear fruit unless you remain in me. I am the vine; you are the branches. If you remain in me and I in you, you will bear much fruit; apart from me you can do nothing. If you do not remain in me, you are like a branch that is thrown away and withers; such branches are picked up, thrown into the fire and burned. (John 15:1-6)

We can only produce good fruit in Christ and anything outside of that produces bad fruit. That includes what we would consider good.

A great deception from the Tree of Knowledge is the 'good'. It is easy enough to recognise the evil is not something to be proud of, but the good part of this tree has blinded us to our true condition. The good mankind produces from our own abilities justifies our self-righteousness. When we feel we have the capability of good, there is no need to be accountable to the Creator. This kind of good has blinded more men and women to God's truth than our open rebellion.

The Tree of Knowledge is appealing.

> When the woman saw that the fruit of the tree was good for food and pleasing to the eye, and also desirable for gaining wisdom... (Genesis 3:6)

The good produced from this tree is nourishing, pleasing and desirable, therefore highly deceptive.

The good produced from the Tree of Knowledge is independent from God, therefore men in their good deeds are led away from God, not toward Him.

Any good produced outside of Christ is not of God. When we are producing good fruit from the Tree of Knowledge, it is still bad fruit. John 15 clearly says, unless that good is produced from the vine (Jesus), it will be pruned or cast into the fire.

The 'rich young ruler' found in Luke 18:18-23 is an excellent example of the pinnacle of man's good not being good enough for God's kingdom. We see a young successful man, who lived a good life. He believed in God, obeyed his parents, was law-abiding and had an influential position within the community. He had all the qualities of life mankind strives for. But these accomplishments came from the Tree of Knowledge and Jesus knew that. He asked this impressive young man to let go of that tree and come and join the true vine. This man could not, because it was too costly for him to let go.

God knows the damage the Tree of Knowledge has had on mankind. Throughout the Bible He teaches us to draw our life from His tree. The book of Romans looks at this influence more intensely than most other books in the Bible.

When we live by the flesh, we are living by the influence of the tree of knowledge, but when we live by the Spirit, we are living by the influence of the True Vine, (Jesus Christ).

> Those who live according to the flesh have their minds set on what the flesh desires; but those who live in accordance with the Spirit have their minds set on what the Spirit desires. The mind governed by the flesh is death, but the mind governed by the Spirit is life and peace. The mind governed by the flesh is hostile to God; it doesn't submit to God's law, nor can it do so. Those who are in the realm of the flesh cannot please God. (Romans 8:5-8)

Everything we do in the flesh comes from the Tree of Knowledge, everything we do in the Spirit, comes from the True Vine, Jesus Christ.

Part 2
Redemption

Chapter 5

The Passover

One of the oldest religious festivals celebrated today is the Jewish Passover. This annual festival is a shadow of something far greater that would change the spiritual dynamics for mankind forever.

> The LORD said to Moses and Aaron in Egypt, 'This month is to be for you the first month, the first month of your year. Tell the whole community of Israel that on the tenth day of this month each man is to take a lamb for his family, one for each household ... The animals you choose must be year-old males without defect, and you may take them from the sheep or the goats. Take care of them until the fourteenth day of the month, when all the members of the community of Israel must slaughter them at twilight. Then they are to take some of the blood and put it on the sides and tops of the doorframes of the houses where they eat the lambs.
>
> 'That same night they are to eat the meat roasted over the fire, along with bitter herbs, and bread made without yeast. Do not eat the meat raw or boiled in water, but roast it over a fire – with the head, legs and internal organs. Do not leave any of it till morning; if some is left till morning, you must burn it. This is how you are to eat it: with your cloak tucked into your belt, your sandals on your feet and your staff in your hand. Eat it in

> haste; it is the LORD's Passover. On that same night I will pass through Egypt and strike down every firstborn of both people and animals, and I will bring judgment on all the gods of Egypt.
>
> 'I am the LORD. The blood will be sign for you on the houses where you are, and when I see the blood, I will pass over you. No destructive plague will touch you when I strike Egypt. This is a day you are to commemorate; for the generations to come you shall celebrate it as a festival to the LORD – a lasting ordinance.' (Exodus 12:1-14)

This Passover Festival was fulfilled when Jesus Christ came into this world as a man, was sentenced by both religious and secular worlds and put to death. But that isn't where it ended, for He rose again and became salvation to all who accept Him as Lord of their lives.

The Passover remains the remembrance of when God freed the Israelites from the bondage of Egypt and sent them to a land that was flowing with milk and honey.

> So I have come down to rescue them from the hand of the Egyptians and to bring them up out of that land into a good and spacious land, a land flowing with milk and honey... (Exodus 3:8)

Christians today celebrate the fulfilment of this Passover, the death and resurrection of Jesus Christ.

The original Jewish Passover celebration was a shadow of what Christ accomplished on the cross. Throughout this festival, we see fundamental truths accomplishing their true fulfilment in Jesus the Messiah. Let us look at some of these truths.

The Passover changed the Israelites New Year.

> The LORD said to Moses and Aaron in Egypt, 'This month

is to be for you the first month, the first month of your year.'
(Exodus 12:1-2)

Just as God was about to create a new beginning for the Israelites, so too does Jesus for all new believers.

> Now there was a Pharisee, a man named Nicodemus who was a member of the Jewish ruling council. He came to Jesus at night and said, 'Rabbi, we know that you are a teacher who has come from God. For no one could perform the signs you are doing if God were not with him.' Jesus replied, 'Very truly I tell you, no one can see the kingdom of God unless they are born again.'
> (John 3:1-3)

When Jesus Christ is accepted as Lord, a new life begins.

> Jesus answered, 'I am the way and the truth and the life. No one comes to the Father except through me.' (John 14:6)

What Jesus is saying here is until we come to Him, we are dead, lost and deceived.

To be born-again means our lives really do start from that point. Being born-again means our lives are directed by the Lord Jesus Christ and not ourselves or anything else.

> Therefore, if anyone is in Christ, the new creation has come. The old has gone, the new is here! (2 Corinthians 5:17)

Another aspect of Passover, the lamb sacrificed was to have no defects.

> The animals you choose must be year-old males without defect,

> and you may take them from the sheep or the goats. (Exodus 12:5)

John the Baptist (who came to prepare the way for Jesus) testified Jesus was to be this Passover lamb.

> The next day John saw Jesus coming toward him and said, 'Look, the Lamb of God, who takes away the sin of the world!' (John 1:29)

Jesus became our perfect sacrifice.

> For you know that it was not with perishable things such as silver of gold that you were redeemed from the empty way of life handed down to you from your ancestors, but with the precious blood of Christ, a lamb without blemish or defect. (1 Peter 1:18-19)

For over 20 years I have graded lambs at a processing plant. Here are some facts about lambs. A lamb is only a lamb for about a year, after that it matures into a hogget. The prime market for ovine is lamb. The lamb is at the prime of its life. Jesus died at the prime of His life. He sacrificed everything for His Father.

A lot of lamb defects are internal, for example, pleurisy, gland infections, internal diseases and many others. It makes sense the Israelites were to examine the lamb or goat for two weeks. Only through close examination would you be able to pick up any internal defects.

> ...but with the precious blood of Christ, a lamb without blemish or defect. (1 Peter 1:19)

> He committed no sin, and no deceit was found in his mouth.
> (1 Peter 2:22)

When God instituted Passover, the details are important. One of these details is the time all Passover lambs had to be sacrificed. The English translations let us down concerning this particular instruction.

The English versions say the lamb must be killed in the evening or at twilight, but this is not what the original Hebrew says. It should read, 'slay it between the two evenings.' This comes from two Hebrew words in verse 6, 'beyn'[5] (which means between) and 'ereb'[6] (which means evening or evenings). Bible scholars have concluded 'between the two evenings' is 3pm.[7] This is the time Jesus died on the cross.

> And at three in the afternoon Jesus cried out in a loud voice …
> With a loud cry, Jesus breathed his last. (Mark 15:34a, 37)

Another powerful picture within Passover is the blood.

> Then they are to take some of the blood and put it on the sides and tops of the doorframes of the houses where they eat the lambs… On that same night I will pass through Egypt and strike down every firstborn of both people and animals, and I will bring judgment on all the gods of Egypt. I am the LORD. The blood will be a sign for you on the houses where you are, and when I see the blood, I will pass over you. No destruc-

---

5 *Strong's Hebrew Lexicon* 996
6 *Strong's Hebrew Lexicon* 6153
7 Heraldmag.org (Time Elements of the Passover: Type and Antitype, by George Tabac)

tive plague will touch you when I strike Egypt. (Exodus 12:7, 12-13)

When Jesus Christ fulfilled this requirement on the cross, His blood represented all the Old Covenant sacrifices.

> In fact, the law requires nearly everything be cleansed with blood, and without the shedding of blood there is no forgiveness. (Hebrews 9:22)

Jesus' sacrificed blood cleanses us of our sin.

> How much more, then, will the blood of Christ, who through the eternal Spirit offered himself unblemished to God, cleanse our consciences from acts that lead to death, so that we may serve the living God! (Hebrews 9:14)

The Passover celebration was a reminder to Israel how God set them free from slavery and brought them out of Egypt. Slavery represents sin and Egypt represents the world. Jesus sets us free from sin and separates us from the world.

> Jesus replied, 'Very truly I tell you, everyone who sins is a slave to sin. Now a slave has no permanent place in the family, but a son belongs to it forever. So if the Son sets you free, you will be free indeed.' (John 8:34-36)

Jesus said in John 7:7, 'The world cannot hate you, but it hates me because I testify that its works are evil.'

> If the world hates you, keep in mind that it hated me first. If you belonged to the world, it would love you as its own. As it

> is, you do not belong to the world, but I have chosen you out of the world. That is why the world hates you. (John 15:18-19)

The world is under the influence of sin and sin hates God. When we come out from under the influence of sin, the world will hate us too.

The Passover was a precursor of what was to come. The Lord Jesus Christ was, and is the fulfilment of this Passover celebration.

There is an astounding truth here even many Christians do not fully comprehend. The second we received Christ, we stepped out of this world and into a found eternity with Christ. We walk in eternity. We can walk in this victory constantly, certain of our place with Him.

It is never about who we are. It is entirely about who He is.

Chapter 6

Repentance

Repentance is important because Jesus spoke about it, John the Baptist preached it and the Apostles, after the death and resurrection of Christ, preached it.

> In those days John the Baptist came, preaching in the wilderness of Judea and saying, 'Repent, for the kingdom of heaven has come near.' (Matthew 3:1-2)

Jesus, from the beginning of His public preaching, preached repentance.

> From that time on Jesus began to preach, 'Repent, for the kingdom of heaven has come near.' (Matthew 4:17)

Jesus sent out His twelve disciples with the message of repentance.

> Calling the Twelve to him, he began to send them out two by two and gave them authority over impure spirits… They went out and preached that people should repent. (Mark 6:7, 6:12)

Jesus said in Luke 13:3, 5, 'I tell you, no! But unless you repent, you too will all perish.'

The first message spoken by the Disciple Peter after the death and resurrection of Jesus was repentance.

> Peter replied, 'Repent and be baptised, every one of you, in the name of Jesus Christ for the forgiveness of your sins. And you will receive the gift of the Holy Spirit.' (Acts 2:38)

The Apostle Paul preached repentance.

> In the past God overlooked such ignorance, but now he commands all people everywhere to repent. (Acts 17:30)

God wants everyone to repent.

> The Lord is not slow in keeping his promise, as some understand slowness. Instead he is patient with you, not wanting anyone to perish, but everyone to come to repentance. (2 Peter 3:9)

What is repentance? Repentance means to change one's mind.[8] That doesn't sound too powerful or convincing for it to be a fundamental requirement, but it is more than just changing one's mind, because the Holy Spirit is involved. It is a spiritual awakening which brings us to a place where we realise our thinking has been wrong concerning Christ Jesus.

When conviction of the Holy Spirit brings repentance, it reaches deep into the heart so real transformation can happen. This is what happened when Peter preached to a crowd of Jews.

> When the people heard this, they were cut to the heart and said to Peter and the other apostles, 'Brothers, what shall we do?'

---

8 *Strong's Lexicon* G3340

> Peter replied, 'Repent and be baptised, every one of you, in the name of Jesus Christ for the forgiveness of your sins. And you will receive the gift of the Holy Spirit.' (Acts 2:37-38)

Repentance requires both yourself and the Holy Spirit to involve the Lord Jesus Christ.

> When he [the Holy Spirit] comes, he will prove the world to be in the wrong about sin and righteousness and judgment: about sin, because people do not believe in me [Jesus Christ]. (John 16:8-9)

It's the asking for forgiveness because we have all fallen short of the glory of God, and the accepting of Jesus Christ as Lord.

> This righteousness is given through faith in Jesus Christ to all who believe. There is no difference between Jew and Gentile, for all have sinned and fall short of the glory of God, and all are justified freely by his grace through the redemption that came by Christ Jesus. (Romans 3:22-24)

Repentance is recognising our failure and Christ's victory. Only through the Lord Jesus Christ can we have victory. It is changing our focus from ourselves and what's around us to fixing our desires on Christ Jesus. Jesus said in John 14:21, 'Whoever has my commands and keeps them is the one who loves me. The one who loves me will be loved by my Father, and I too will love them and show myself to them.'

The ability to repent is a gift from God, reflecting the ability to choose. As early as Genesis 1:27 we are told we are made 'in His own image'. This likeness to God is seen in our ability to choose. Animals don't choose. They operate by instinct.

Man alone can choose to forgive, can choose love over hate, life over death, to receive Christ or not, just as he chose to partake of the fruit from the Tree of Knowledge. The ability to choose has a supernatural power beyond our imagining.

Chapter 7

Born-again

It is only through Jesus Christ we can be redeemed.

How do we know we belong to the Kingdom of God? How can we be sure of our salvation? Jesus gives us the answer in John 3:5-6.

> Jesus answered, 'Very truly I tell you, no one can enter the kingdom of God unless they are born of water and the Spirit. Flesh gives birth to flesh, but the Spirit gives birth to spirit.'

When we repent and accept Jesus Christ as Lord, an amazing thing happens. 'Spirit gives birth to spirit.' The Holy Spirit comes into us and makes our spirit alive to Christ.

> Now it is God who makes both us and you stand firm in Christ. He anointed us, set his seal of ownership on us, and put his Spirit in our hearts as a deposit, guaranteeing what is to come. (2 Corinthians 1:21-22)

> And you also were included in Christ when you heard the message of truth, the gospel of your salvation. When you believed, you were marked in him with a seal, the promised Holy Spirit, who is a deposit guaranteeing our inheritance until the redemp-

tion of those who are God's possession – to the praise of his glory. (Ephesians 1:13-14)

As Christians, there is no doubt we belong to God because the Holy Spirit is present. It is the Holy Spirit who awakens our spirit, therefore deep inside of us, there is a desire to please Jesus Christ. We are walking in blessing, in eternity. Our spirit witnesses with His Spirit. The desire of Holy Spirit within us is for life, not self.

Before I became a Christian my will wanted to please myself, but when I submitted to Christ, my will wants to please Him. My spirit is alive to Christ, wanting to honour Him. It is my flesh that isn't so pleased.

The Holy Spirit is not inactive. If He resides within there will always be an acknowledgement Jesus Christ is Lord and we should honour Him.

If you believe you are a Christian, but there is no desire within you that wants to change from the old way of life, I doubt the Holy Spirit is present and if the Spirit is not present, you are not a Christian.

When the Holy Spirit is present, there is a deep acknowledgement you belong to God.

> Because you are his sons, God sent the Spirit of his Son into our hearts, the Spirit who calls out, 'Abba, Father.' (Galatians 4:6)

Our heart is able to cry out, 'God, you are my Heavenly Father. Jesus, You are my Lord.' This is important to know because this becomes our driving force.

> Whoever believes in me, as Scripture has said, rivers of living water will flow from within them. (John 7:38)

This is the Holy Spirit who dwells within.

There lies within us a desire to honour Jesus Christ beyond the Sunday Service. If there is no driving desire within to honour Jesus Christ, this puts a big question mark on whether we are Christian or not.

Chapter 8

Redemption Prophesied – The Redeemer Foretold

No book in human history has accurately predicted one event so many times, hundreds of years before it happened. No book in human history accurately predicts a Messiah who would bring redemption hundreds of years before he was born, except the Bible.

There are many prophecies and similitudes in the Old Testament and a section of these centre on the death and resurrection of Jesus Christ. It so successfully does it many critics have accused the Bible (the Old Testament) of being tampered with, claiming these prophecies were added after Jesus died on the cross.

One of many historical facts proving the Bible wasn't tampered with is the Septuagint. This Greek translation of the Hebrew Old Testament was translated between 300-200 BC,[9] hundreds of years before Jesus Christ was born. When Jesus was born, this version was widely used by the Jews. Jesus and the disciples frequently quoted from it.

The Septuagint was again proven to be accurate between AD 1947 and 1956, when the Dead Sea Scrolls were discovered. The Dead Sea Scrolls are the oldest group of Old Testament manuscripts ever found.[10] And they were written in Hebrew.

---

9   www.septuagint.net
10 www.centuryone.com/25dssfacts.html

When the Septuagint was compared against these manuscripts, it was an accurate account of the Old Testament with only minor grammatical differences, which did not change the message portrayed.

If you are still not sure about the authenticity of the Old Testament, do some serious historical research. Don't be influenced by shallow opinions of people who haven't done their homework. The Old and New Testaments will always remain true, no matter how meticulously scrutinised.

The Old Testament contains many prophecies and pictures of Jesus Christ. There are stories in the Old Testament that don't make much sense, but become clearer through the death and resurrection of Christ. There are also types of Christ portrayed through different characters in the Bible. The Old Testament is full of prophecies, types and similitudes of Christ.

To look into all the different portrayals of Christ in the Old Testament would require many books. We will look at a few examples of prophecy, types and pictures specifically centred on redemption. And we will look at the first book of the Bible, Genesis.

This will show how Jesus was able to walk with two disciples for about seven miles and tell them what was said in all the scriptures concerning the death and resurrection of Himself (Luke 24:13-32).

Let's look at this redemption story in the book of Genesis. Beginning with Genesis 1:1-3,

> In the beginning God created the heavens and the earth. Now the earth was formless and empty, darkness was over the surface of the deep, and the Spirit of God was hovering over the waters. And God said, 'Let there be light,' and there was light.

From the beginning of Scripture, we see a continuing pattern emerging. The pattern of redemption, God brings light into the darkness. Jesus is the true light.

> In the beginning was the Word, and the Word was with God, and the Word was God. He was with God in the beginning. Through him all things were made; without him nothing was made that has been made. In him was life, and that life was the light of all mankind. (John 1:1-4)

Redemption brings us into the true light.

> ...and giving joyful thanks to the Father, who has qualified you to share in the inheritance of his holy people in the kingdom of light. For he has rescued us from the dominion of darkness and brought us into the kingdom of the Son he loves, in whom we have redemption, the forgiveness of sins. (Colossians 1:12-14)

The next redemptive scripture in Genesis is the first prophecy concerning the death and resurrection of Jesus Christ.

It's found in Genesis 3:15,

> And I will put enmity between thee and the woman, and between thy seed and her seed; it shall bruise thy head, and thou shalt bruise his heel. (KJV)

This verse deserves extensive exegesis (for example, how the devil tried to contaminate and then destroy the Messianic seed), but let's concentrate on the redemptive aspects. This verse has Satan bruising Jesus' feet, but Jesus crushes Satan's head.

The bruising of Jesus' feet is the suffering He endured throughout His life on earth. It becomes much more intense when it is centred on the cross.

> Many bulls have compassed me: strong bulls of Bashan have beset me around. They gaped upon me with their mouths, as a

ravening and a roaring lion. I am poured out like water, and all my bones are out of joint: my heart is like wax; it is melted in the midst of my bowels. My strength is dried up like a potsherd; and my tongue cleaveth to my jaws; and thou hast brought me into the dust of death. For dogs have compassed me: the assembly of the wicked have enclosed me: they pierced my hands and my feet. (Psalm 22:12-16 KJV)

This is one of the prophecies giving specific details of what the Messiah would experience on the cross.

At the cross we see the human accusers; the religious rulers and the Roman soldiers carrying out the death sentence, and often animals mentioned (strong bulls, roaring lion, dogs) are referred to as humans surrounding the cross.

But we must remember that the real accusers go deeper than human influence. Satan and his ilk, or evil spirits, were the main force; 'behind the scenes'. Often overlooked at the cross, these evil spirits must have thought they were witnessing a great victory.

I suggest here the Bible records three realms of Satan's gloating kingdom.

The bulls of Bashan represent powerful fallen angels. These angels set themselves up as gods, principalities, strongholds, beings of enlightenment and many other positions of influence, to be worshipped and obeyed.

For example, Molech, which was represented by a bronze statue with a head of a bull and demanded child sacrifice. You may be surprised the worship of this ancient detestable god,[11] is still practised in Western society today. And few realise the term Good Luck comes directly from the word Molech.

We see in this Psalm, these fallen angels are acting on behalf of

---

11 Leviticus 18:21, 20:2-5, 1 Kings 11:7, 2 Kings 23:10, Jeremiah 32:35.

their master; Satan. That's why we see in the verse bulls acting like raging lions.

> Be alert and of sober mind. Your enemy the devil prowls around like a roaring lion looking for someone to devour. (1 Peter 5:8)

And no doubt, the devil himself would have been present. I guess that's why the bulls of Bashan were roaring like lions - trying to impress their master.

The dogs surrounding Jesus could represent demons sent to oppress and possess humans.

We see a picture of the satanic kingdom gathering around Jesus, gloating, accusing and believing they were winning a victory, but in all their efforts, they could only bruise His heel.

Jesus however, bruises the devil's head. The head represents power and authority and when Jesus died and rose again, this was a powerful blow against the satanic kingdom. Through Jesus, the power the devil has over mankind was broken.

> Since the children have flesh and blood, he too shared in their humanity so that by his death he might break the power of him who holds the power of death – that is, the devil – and free those who all their lives were held in slavery by their fear of death. (Hebrews 2:14-15)

Jesus came to destroy the devil's work,

> The one who does what is sinful is of the devil, because the devil has been sinning from the beginning. The reason the Son of God appeared was to destroy the devil's work. (1 John 3:8)

Jesus was triumphant over the satanic kingdom.

> And having disarmed the powers and authorities, he made a public spectacle of them, triumphing over them by the cross. (Colossians 2:15)

As Genesis 3:15 shows, Satan could only bruise Jesus' heel, yet Jesus crushed Satan's head.

In Genesis, we find the first sacrifice made,

> Unto Adam also and to his wife did the LORD God make coats of skins, and clothed them. (Genesis 3:21 KJV)

Through this sacrifice, God clothed Adam and Eve. It is important to note the first sacrifice mentioned in the Bible was initiated by God, not man. And it was in an act of mercy, and forgiveness.

The death and resurrection of Christ was initiated by the Triune God. Man can take no credit for what was accomplished on the cross. The clothing of Adam and Eve goes beyond mere clothing. We are clothed through the sacrifice of Christ.

> So in Christ Jesus you are all children of God through faith, for all of you who were baptised into Christ have clothed yourselves with Christ. (Galatians 3:26-27)

The sacrifice of animals was a requirement of the Old Testament, Jesus fulfils all requirements once and for all at the cross.

> But when Christ came as high priest to the good things that are now already here, he went through the greater and more perfect tabernacle that is not made with human hands, that is to say, is not a part of this creation. He did not enter by means of the blood of goats and calves; but he entered the Most Holy

Place once and for all by his own blood, thus obtaining eternal redemption.

The blood of goats and bulls and the ashes of a heifer sprinkled on those who are ceremonially unclean sanctify them so that they are outwardly clean. How much more, then, will the blood of Christ, who through the eternal Spirit offered himself unblemished to God, cleanse our consciences from acts that lead to death so that we may serve the living God. (Hebrews 9:11-14)

The next example is a type of Christ found in Genesis 4:3-8, the story of Cain and Abel. Abel was a righteous man, but Cain's actions were evil.

Do not be like Cain, who belonged to the evil one and murdered his brother. And why did he murder him? Because his own actions were evil and his brother's were righteous. (1 John 3:12)

Jesus came as a righteous man, but suffered death because of the sins of mankind.

For Christ also suffered once for sins, the righteous for the unrighteous, to bring you to God. He was put to death in the body but made alive in the Spirit. (1 Peter 3:18)

Just as Abel was killed by his brother, so too was Jesus betrayed and killed by His Jewish brothers.

Then the Pharisees went out and began to plot with the Herodians how they might kill Jesus. (Mark 3:6)

God's Way to Success

Just like Cain, the Pharisees, Sadducees and the religious rulers who opposed Jesus, were rejected by God, while Jesus was accepted. Their hearts became filled with hatred and rage and murder filled their thoughts. When sin takes hold, it puts to death God's righteous workings in our lives. In the same way, God's Word is death to the unbeliever. The 'self spirit' of the unbeliever know it is perishing, lost to eternity.

Another great example of redemption is the genealogical names from Adam to Noah in Genesis 5:1-29. The meaning of their names paints a brilliant picture of man's despair and Christ's redemptive hope. Because of the details needed to portray it, the next chapter will look at this.

Another example is the story of Noah and the Ark (Genesis 6:8-8:22), which is a very clear picture of exclusive salvation.

> For Christ also suffered once for sins, the righteous for the unrighteous, to bring you to God. He was put to death in the body but made alive in the Spirit. After being made alive, he went and made proclamation to the imprisoned spirits – to those who were disobedient long ago when God waited patiently in the days of Noah while the ark was being built. In it only a few people, eight in all, were saved through water, and this water symbolises the baptism that now saves you also – not the removal of dirt from the body but the pledge of a clear conscience toward God.
>
> It saves you by the resurrection of Jesus Christ, who has gone into heaven and is at God's right hand – with angels, authorities and powers in submission to him. (1 Peter 3:18-22)

Anyone who was not on the ark, died. There was no other way to survive, if you were not in the ark, you perished in the flood.

Jesus is our Ark. Anyone who rejects the Lordship of Jesus over their lives, will perish.

> Jesus answered, 'I am the way and the truth and the life. No one comes to the Father except through me.' (John 14:6)

> For God did not send his Son into the world to condemn the world, but to save the world through him. Whoever believes in him is not condemned, but whoever does not believe stands condemned already because they have not believed in the name of God's one and only Son. (John 3:17-18)

There is only one guide who leads us to heaven, and his name is Jesus Christ.

Abraham is another example. There are two prophetic pictures portrayed in the life of Abraham. The first is found in Genesis 15:13-14,

> Then the LORD said to him, 'Know for certain that for four hundred years your descendants will be strangers in a country not their own and that they will be enslaved and mistreated there. But I will punish the nation they serve as slaves, and afterward they will come out with great possessions.'

This event was covered in the first chapter of this section. This Passover Festival was eventually fulfilled when Jesus Christ died and rose again on the cross, triumphing over His enemies.

> And having disarmed the powers and authorities, he made a public spectacle of them, triumphing over them by the cross. (Colossians 2:15)

We need to take notice of God's timing. He prophesies precisely to Abraham how long the Israelites will be in Egypt and when they will be released, which is 400 years. The New Testament declares it was God's timing when Jesus came to this earth to deliver mankind.

> But when the set time had fully come, God sent his Son, born of a woman, born under the law, to redeem those under the law, that we might receive adoption to sonship. (Galatians 4:4-5)

The second prophetic picture concerning Abraham is found in Genesis 22:1-19. It is when God tells Abraham to sacrifice his son Isaac. This story goes against God's standard where He abhors human sacrifice practised by pagan nations.

It also doesn't make sense because Isaac was promised to be the father of nations, especially His Chosen Nation. This story only makes full sense when Jesus was crucified in the same region many, many years later.

God is prophetically telling the story of what His Only Begotten Son will have to go through in the future.

> Then God said, 'Take your son, your only son, whom you love – Isaac – and go to the region of Moriah. Sacrifice him there as a burnt offering on a mountain I will show you.' (Genesis 22:2)

> For God so loved the world, that he gave his only begotten Son, that whosoever believeth in him should not perish, but have everlasting life. (John 3:16 KJV)

Jesus speaks of His own death.

> 'We are going up to Jerusalem, and the Son of Man will be delivered over to the chief priests and the teachers of the law.

They will condemn him to death and will hand him over to the Gentiles to be mocked and flogged and crucified. On the third day he will be raised to life!' (Matthew 20:18-19)

The obedience of Abraham here is remarkable. He trusted that God knew what He was doing, even if he didn't. And Abraham answers prophetically, when asked by his son Isaac, 'But where is the lamb for the burnt offering?'

And Abraham said, My son, God will provide himself a lamb for a burnt offering. (Genesis 22:8 KJV)

Over 2000 years later God Himself came as the sacrifice.

Have the same mindset as Christ Jesus: Who, being in very nature God, did not consider equality with God something to be used to his own advantage; rather, he made himself nothing by taking the very nature of a servant, being made in human likeness. And being found in appearance as a man, he humbled himself by becoming obedient to death – even death on a cross! (Philippians 2:5b-8)

He came as the sacrificial Lamb.

The next day John saw Jesus coming toward him and said, 'Look, the Lamb of God, who takes away the sin of the world!' (John 1:29)

Even though a ram was provided by God for Abraham to sacrifice instead of his son, over 2000 years later in the same spot, God did not spare His own Son.

Then he said to them, 'My soul is overwhelmed with sorrow to the point of death. Stay here and keep watch with me.'

Going a little farther, he fell with his face to the ground and prayed, 'My Father, if it is possible, may this cup be taken from me. Yet not as I will, but as you will.' ...He went away a second time and prayed. 'My Father, if it is not possible for this cup to be taken away unless I drink it, may your will be done.' (Matthew 26:38-39, 42)

He who did not spare his own Son, but gave him up for us all... (Romans 8:32a)

Herein is love, not that we loved God, but that he loved us, and sent his Son to be the propitiation for our sins. (1 John 4:10 KJV)

The story of Abraham and Isaac is more than a test of Abraham's love toward God, it was God's prophetic picture of His love toward mankind.

Another example is the life of Joseph found in Genesis chapters 37 through to chapter 50. This is a miraculous story of betrayal and salvation. The story of Joseph is a picture of what Jesus suffered and accomplished on the cross.

Joseph's favour by his father stirred up jealousy amongst his brothers. They hated him even more when he told them of dreams he had where they and his parents would bow down to him. They plotted to kill him (Genesis 37:4-11, 18-20).

Jesus reveals His true authority to the Jewish religious leaders,

'Very truly I tell you,' Jesus answered, 'before Abraham was born I am!' (John 8:58)

Jesus reveals His true identity,

> 'I and the Father are one.' (John 10:30)

This amongst many other things Jesus said and did, made the Jews who opposed Him very angry, filled with hatred, they wanted to kill Him.

> And the Pharisees went out and began to plot with the Herodians how they might kill Jesus. (Mark 3:6)

Jesus is condemned by His Jewish brothers to death.

> It was the day of Preparation of the Passover; it was about noon. 'Here is your king,' Pilate said to the Jews. But they shouted, 'Take him away! Take him away! Crucify him!' (John 19:14-15a)

Another example in the story of Joseph, is the condition mankind needs to be, before salvation. While Joseph was in Egypt, he interpreted the Pharaoh's prophetic dream which was seven years of plenty, then seven years of famine for Egypt and the surrounding nations. It was only during the famine did Joseph's brothers go down to Egypt to buy food. Joseph's family were destitute and in need.

A broken and contrite heart is the cause of our need for Christ.

> Blessed are the poor in spirit, for theirs is the kingdom of heaven. Blessed are those who mourn, for they will be comforted. Blessed are the meek, for they will inherit the earth. Blessed are those who hunger and thirst for righteousness, for they will be filled. (Matthew 5:3-6)

Only when we realise our spiritual famine and come to Jesus Christ for our nourishment, do we experience true salvation.

The story of Joseph ends triumphantly. He is able to save not only his family, but other nations from famine (Genesis 41:53-57).

> He told them, 'This is what is written: The Messiah will suffer and rise from the dead on the third day, and repentance for the forgiveness of sins will be preached in his name to all nations, beginning at Jerusalem.' (Luke 24:46-47)

> Then Jesus came to them and said, 'All authority in heaven and on earth has been given to me. Therefore go and make disciples of all nations, baptising them in the name of the Father and of the Son and of the Holy Spirit, and teaching them to obey everything I have commanded you. And surely I am with you always, to the very end to the age.' (Matthew 28:18-20)

Chapter 9

The Redemptive Story – From Adam to Noah

The genealogy from Adam to Noah is not just a factual account in history, it has the redemptive pattern built into it.[12]

> This is the book of the generations of Adam. In the day that God created man, in the likeness of God made he him. (Genesis 5:1 KJV)

Genesis 5:1-30 records the genealogical line of Adam through to Noah. These are the names: Adam, Seth, Enos, Kenan, Mahalalel, Jared, Enoch, Methuselah, Lamech, Noah.

Each of these names has a meaning, when you put these meanings together in order of birth, starting with Adam and ending with Noah, the redemptive picture emerges. Starting with Adam, we will look at the meaning of their names.

Adam[13] means man, mankind or human. It also means colour of the earth. So together, it becomes, man of the earth.

Seth's meaning is best described by Eve.

---

12 I first heard this picture of redemption from Chuck Missler of Koinonia House, but the final picture portrayed is my own research.
13 *Zondervan Exhaustive Concordance*, (Hebrew to English 132, 134)

> And Adam knew his wife; and she bore a son, and called his name Seth: For God, said she, hath appointed me another seed instead of Abel, whom Cain slew. (Genesis 4:25 KJV)

Seth means appointed.

Enos or Enosh means mortal man, with an emphasis on frailty.[14] Enosh comes from the Hebraic root words *anash* and *'nsh*.[15] *Anash* means to be weak or sick. *'Nsh*, when it is used in the name *'enosh*, means man or mankind. Enosh means, mankind, mortal and frail.

Cainan or Kenan comes from the Hebrew word *Qenan* which is strongly believed[16] to come from the verb (*qin*), meaning to chant a dirge. And this verb comes from the noun (*qina*), meaning lamentation, or a sad poem which is sung. Kenan also means nest, taken from the Hebraic root word *qen*.[17] Now this particular nest refers to the eagle's nest high in the cliffs out of reach. Kenan means, sorrow, destitution and an eagle's nest.

Mahalalel needs to be split in two, Mahalal and El. Mahalal or *halal* means praise. *El*, which is an abbreviation for *Elohim*, means God. Mahalalel means praise of God.[18]

Jared comes from the Hebrew words, *Yarad* and *Yered*.[19] *Yarad* means to descend, to go down, or to go from a place of nobility to a place of lower status. *Yered* means servant. Jared means, descend and servant.

---

14 *Zondervan Exhaustive Concordance*, (Hebrew to English 632)
15 Abarim Publications (Etymology of the name Enosh)
16 Abarim Publications (Etymology of the name Kenan)
17 *Strong's Lexicon* H7077
18 *Strong's Lexicon* H4111. Abarim Publications (Etymology of the name Mahalalel)
19 *Zondervan Exhaustive Concordance*, (Hebrew to English 3718, 3719)

Enoch comes from the Hebraic root word *hanak*.[20] The noun means mouth, but this came from the practice of midwives rubbing the palate of a baby's mouth with chewed dates, this was to teach them to suck. The verb came out of this practice, meaning; to inaugurate, train, dedicate or to initiate. The adjective *hanik* means trained or experienced. Enoch means, teach us.

Methuselah is three words, *met, hu, selah*. Met comes from the Hebraic root words *mat* and *mut*.[21] *Mat* denotes a male capable of combat. *Mut* in its root-verb means, to die or to kill. The nouns derived from this verb always involves death. *Hu* or *huw* means he, she, it.[22] Selah comes from the Hebraic root word *shalah*, which means to send. It also frequently describes God sending someone.

There is the Hebraic masculine noun s*helah*, which denotes some kind of weapon like a javelin or dart. Add that with *mat*, which means a man capable of combat, you start to see why Methuselah is often translated, 'man of the dart or man of a javelin.'

But when we take note of the most common translations within his name, we see another picture emerge. Methuselah means; a capable man died, he was sent by God.

Lamech[23] is two words, la and mech. La comes from the Hebraic root word *le*. *Le* is simply a preposition, it leads us toward or into the actual word. Mech comes from the Hebraic root verbs, *makak* and *muk*.

They both mean to be low or humiliated. *Makak* refers to the bringing down because of sin, or the bringing down into netherworld of death. *Muk* is used to denote an impoverished nation.

---

20 Abarim Publications (Etymology of the name Enoch)
21 Abarim Publications (Etymology of the name Methuselah)
22 *Strong's Lexicon* H1931
23 Abarim Publications (Etymology of the name Lamech)

So Lamech could mean, 'have become a nation impoverished and heading to hell.'

Noah means rest, comfort.[24] Other studies researching the name of Noah however, have led to other root words. Noah could have derived from the root verbs, *muah, nahet,* and *naha*.[25] *Muah* means rest, or coming to the end of a journey and resting, or a general peace of mind. It may also mean, to leave behind. *Nahet* means to descend or go down. It may denote a military advance, or a descent into Sheol (the netherworld of death). *Naha* means to lead or to guide.

With all the names and their meanings from Adam through to Noah, we can link the meanings together and see a wonderful picture of God's redemption through His Son emerge.

Adam, Seth, Enos, Cainan, Mahalalel, Jared, Enoch, Methuselah, Lamech, Noah, seen in this order, through the meaning of their names, we get something like this:-

'Man of the earth, you have been appointed mortality, frailty, sorrow and destitution. You have built nests away from Me. But praise be to God who descended from a place of nobility to become a servant. This was initiated by God to teach us this capable man was sent to die for the nations, which are impoverished and heading to hell. He descended into Sheol with authority to confront his enemy and now leads and guides us to rest and comfort.'

---

24 *Zondervan Exhaustive Concordance* (Hebrew to English 5695)
25 Abarim Publications (Etymology of the name Noah)

Chapter 10

Isaiah 53

Isaiah 53 is one of the best descriptions of the suffering Messiah. The best commentary this chapter deserves is not man's commentary, but commentary by the Bible itself. This chapter will quote Isaiah 53 which sees its fulfilment in New Testament verses.

> Who has believed our message and to whom has the arm of the LORD been revealed? (Isaiah 53:1)

> He was in the world, and the world was made by him, and the world knew him not. He came unto his own, and his own received him not. But as many as received him, to them gave he power to become the sons of God, even to them that believe on his name: Which were born, not of blood, nor of the will of the flesh, nor of the will of man, but of God. (John 1:10-13 KJV)

> But not all the Israelites accepted the good news. For Isaiah says, 'Lord, who has believed our message?' Consequently, faith comes from hearing the message, and the message is heard through the word about Christ. (Romans 10:16-17)

> He grew up before him like a tender shoot, and like a root out of dry ground. He had not beauty or majesty to attract us

to him, nothing in his appearance that we should desire him. (Isaiah 53:2)

So Joseph also went up from the town of Nazareth in Galilee to Judea, to Bethlehem the town of David, because he belonged to the house and line of David. He went there to register with Mary, who was pledged to be married to him and was expecting a child. While they were there, the time came for the baby to be born, and she gave birth to her firstborn, a son. She wrapped him in cloths and placed him in a manger, because there was no guest room available for them. (Luke 2:4-7)

For unto you is born this day in the city of David a Saviour, which is Christ the Lord. (Luke 2:11 KJV)

In your relationships with one another, have the same mindset as Christ Jesus: Who, being in very nature God, did not consider equality with God something to be used to his own advantage; rather, he made himself nothing by taking the very nature of a servant, being made in human likeness. And being found in appearance as a man, he humbled himself by becoming obedient to death – even death on a cross! (Philippians 2:5-8)

He was despised and rejected by mankind, a man of suffering, and familiar with pain. Like one from whom people hide their faces he was despised, and we held him in low esteem. (Isaiah 53:3)

Though he were a Son, yet learned he obedience by the things which he suffered. (Hebrews 5:8 KJV)

Isaiah 53

But first he must suffer many things and be rejected by this generation. (Luke 17:25)

And he said, 'The Son of Man must suffer many things and be rejected by the elders, the chief priests and the teachers of the law, and he must be killed and on the third day be raised to life.' (Luke 9:22)

Those who passed by hurled insults at him, shaking their heads and saying, 'So! You who are going to destroy the temple and build it in three days, come down from the cross and save yourself!'
In the same way the chief priests and the teachers of the law mocked him among themselves. 'He saved others,' they said, 'but he can't save himself! Let this Messiah, this king of Israel, come down now from the cross, that we may see and believe.' Those crucified with him also heaped insults on him. (Mark 15:29-32)

Surely he took up our pain and bore our suffering, yet we considered him punished by God, stricken by him, and afflicted. (Isaiah 53:4)

When evening came, many who were demon-possessed were brought to him, and he drove out the spirits with a word and healed all the sick. This was to fulfil what was spoken through the prophet Isaiah: 'He took up our infirmities and bore our diseases.' (Matthew 8:16-17)

Then he said to them, 'My soul is overwhelmed with sorrow to the point of death. Stay here and keep watch with me.' Going a little farther, he fell with his face to the ground and prayed, 'My

Father, if it is possible, may this cup be taken from me. Yet not as I will, but as you will.' (Matthew 26:38-39)

About three in the afternoon Jesus cried out in a loud voice, 'Eli, Eli, lemasabachthani?' ('My God, my God, why have you forsaken me?') (Matthew 27:46)

But he was pierced for our transgressions, he was crushed for our iniquities; the punishment that brought us peace was on him, and by his wounds we are healed. (Isaiah 53:5)

Then they spit in his face and struck him with their fists. Others slapped him and said, 'Prophecy to us, Messiah. Who hit you?' (Matthew 26:67-68)

Then the governor's soldiers took Jesus into the Praetorium and gathered the whole company of soldiers around him. They stripped him and put a scarlet robe on him, and then twisted together a crown of thorns and set it on his head. They put a staff in his right hand.

Then they knelt in front of him and mocked him. 'Hail, king of the Jews!' they said. They spit on him, and took the staff and struck him on the head again and again. After they had mocked him, they took off the robe and put his clothes on him. Then they led him away to crucify him. (Matthew 27:27-31)

When they hurled their insults at him, he did not retaliate; when he suffered, he made no threats. Instead, he entrusted himself to him who judges justly. 'He himself bore our sins' in his body on the cross, so that we might die to sins and live for righteousness; 'by his wounds you have been healed.' (1 Peter 2:23-24)

Isaiah 53

Instead, one of the soldiers pierced Jesus's side with a spear, bringing a sudden flow of blood and water. (John 19:34)

God made him who had no sin to be sin for us, so that in him we might become the righteousness of God. (2 Corinthians 5:21)

He was delivered over to death for our sins and was raised to life for our justification. (Romans 4:25)

We all, like sheep, have gone astray, each of us has turned to our own way; and the LORD has laid on him the iniquity of us all. (Isaiah 53:6)

As it is written: 'There is no one righteous, not even one; there is no one who understands; there is no one who seeks God. All have turned away, they have together become worthless; there is no one who does good, not even one.' (Romans 3:10-12)

When Jesus landed and saw a large crowd, he had compassion on them, because they were like sheep without a shepherd. So he began teaching them many things. (Mark 6:34)

For 'you were like sheep going astray,' but now you have returned to the Shepherd and Overseer of your souls. (1 Peter 2:25)

Herein is love, not that we loved God, but that he loved us, and sent his Son to be the propitiation for our sins. (1 John 4:10 KJV)

He was oppressed and afflicted, yet he did not open his mouth; he was led like a lamb to the slaughter, and as a sheep before its shearers is silent, so he did not open his mouth. (Isaiah 53:7)

This is the passage of Scripture the eunuch was reading: 'He was led like a sheep to the slaughter, and as a lamb before its shearer is silent, so he did not open his mouth.' ...The eunuch asked Philip, 'Tell me, please, who is the prophet talking about, himself or someone else?' Then Philip began with that very passage of Scripture and told him the good news about Jesus. (Acts 8:32, 34-35)

The next day John saw Jesus coming toward him and said, 'Look, the Lamb of God, who takes away the sin of the world!' (John 1:29)

Then the high priest stood up and said to Jesus, 'Are you not going to answer? What is this testimony that these men are bringing against you?' But Jesus remained silent. (Matthew 26:62-63a)

When he was accused by the chief priests and the elders, he gave no answer. Then Pilate asked him, 'Don't you hear the testimony they are bringing against you?' But Jesus made no reply, not even to a single charge – to the great amazement of the governor. (Matthew 27:12-14)

By oppression and judgment he was taken away. Yet who of his generation protested? For he was cut off from the land of the living; for the transgression of my people he was punished. (Isaiah 53:8)

But the chief priests and elders persuaded the multitude that they should ask Barabbas, and destroy Jesus. (Matthew 27:20 KJV)

It was the day of Preparation of the Passover; it was about noon.

Isaiah 53

'Here is your king,' Pilate said to the Jews. But they shouted, 'Take him away! Take him away! Crucify him!' 'Shall I crucify your king?' Pilate asked. 'We have no king but Caesar,' the chief priests answered. Finally Pilate handed him over to them to be crucified. So the soldiers took charge of Jesus. (John 19:14-16)

Then released he Barabbas unto them: and when he had scourged Jesus, he delivered him to be crucified. (Matthew 27:26 KJV)

For as Jonah was three days and three nights in the belly of a huge fish, so the Son of Man will be three days and three nights in the heart of the earth. (Matthew 12:40)

Verily, verily, I say unto you, Except a corn of wheat fall into the ground and die, it abideth alone: but if it die, it bringeth forth much fruit. (John 12:24 KJV)

And I, if I be lifted up from the earth, will draw all men unto me. This he said, signifying what death he should die. (John 12:32-33)

He was delivered over to death for our sins and was raised to life for our justification. (Romans 4:25)

Therefore my heart is glad and my tongue rejoices, my body also will rest in hope, because you will not abandon me to the realm of the dead, you will not let your holy one see decay. (Acts 2:26-27)

For Christ also suffered once for sins, the righteous for the unrighteous, to bring you to God. He was put to death in the body but made alive in the Spirit. (1 Peter 3:18)

He was assigned a grave with the wicked, and with the rich in his death, though he had done no violence, nor was any deceit in his mouth. (Isaiah 53:9)

Two rebels were crucified with him, one on his right and one on his left. (Matthew 27:38)

Christ hath redeemed us from the curse of the law, being made a curse for us: for it is written, Cursed is every one that hangeth on a tree. (Galatians 3:13 KJV)[26]

Now there was a man named Joseph, a member of the Council, a good and upright man, who had not consented to their decision and action. He came from the Judean town of Arimathea, and he himself was waiting for the kingdom of God.
　Going to Pilate, he asked for Jesus' body. Then he took it down, wrapped it in linen cloth and placed it in a tomb cut in the rock, one in which no one had yet been laid. (Luke 23:50-53)

He committed no sin, and no deceit was found in his mouth. (1 Peter 2:22)

Yet it was the LORD's will to crush him and cause him to suffer, and though the LORD makes his life an offering for sin, he will see his offspring and prolong his days, and the will of the LORD will prosper in his hand. (Isaiah 53:10)

And he is the propitiation for our sins: and not for ours only, but also for the sins of the whole world. (1 John 2:2 KJV)

---

26 Deuteronomy 21:22-23

But he has appeared once for all at the culmination of the ages to do away with sin by the sacrifice of himself. Just as people are destined to die once, and after that to face judgement, so Christ was sacrificed once to take away the sins of many; and he will appear a second time, not to bear sin, but to bring salvation to those who are waiting for him. (Hebrews 9:26b-28)

After he has suffered, he will see the light of life and be satisfied; by his knowledge my righteous servant will justify many, and he will bear their iniquities. (Isaiah 53:11)

Whom God hath set forth to be a propitiation through faith in his blood, to declare his righteousness for the remission of sins that are past, through the forbearance of God. To declare, I say, at this time his righteousness: that he might be just, and the justifier of him which believeth in Jesus. (Romans 3:25-26 KJV)

God presented Christ as a sacrifice of atonement, through the shedding of his blood – to be received by faith. He did this to demonstrate his righteousness, because in his forbearance he had left the sins committed beforehand unpunished – he did it to demonstrate his righteousness at the present time, so as to be just and the one who justifies those who have faith in Jesus. (Romans 3:25-26)

Therefore I will give him a portion among the great, and he will divide the spoils with the strong, because he poured out his life unto death, and was numbered with the transgressors. For he bore the sin of many, and made intercession for the transgressors. (Isaiah 53:12)

In your relationships with one another, have the same mindset as Christ Jesus: Who, being in very nature God, did not consider equality with God something to be used to his own advantage; rather, he made himself nothing by taking the very nature of a servant, being made in human likeness. And being found in appearance as a man, he humbled himself by becoming obedient to death – even death on a cross!

Therefore God exalted him to the highest place and gave him the name that is above every name, that at the name of Jesus every knee should bow, in heaven and on earth and under the earth, and every tongue acknowledge that Jesus Christ is Lord, to the glory of God the Father. (Philippians 2:5-11)

Chapter 11

Jonah

Jonah's story connects with the redemption of Christ.

> For as Jonah was a sign to the Ninevites, so also will the Son of Man be to this generation. (Luke 11:30)

> He answered, 'A wicked and adulterous generation asks for a sign! But none will be given it except the sign of the prophet Jonah. For as Jonah was three days and three nights in the belly of a huge fish, so the Son of Man will be three days and three nights in the heart of the earth. The men of Nineveh will stand up at the judgement with this generation and condemn it; for they repented at the preaching of Jonah, and now something greater than Jonah is here.' (Matthew 12:39-41)

The wondrous fact about Bible stories: there is usually more there than we first realise. As we take a closer look we discover truths that paint a clearer picture of Christ, and a clearer picture of man and the Old Covenant law.

There are three important aspects.
First, '…Jonah was a sign to the Ninevites…'
Second, '…three days and three nights in the heart of the huge

fish, so the Son of Man will be three days and three nights in the heart of the earth.'

Third, '...now something greater than Jonah is here.'

First, Jonah was a sign to the Ninevites.

God tells Jonah to go to Nineveh, warning them God's wrath will come upon them in 40 days if they don't repent of their evil. Jonah refuses and gets on a ship going the opposite way. God stirs up a storm threatening all lives on board. To appease God, Jonah is thrown off the ship. God saves him by sending a huge fish to eat him. Within the belly he changes his mind and goes to Nineveh. Nineveh hears the warning and repents.

A wonderful story of an undeserving and wicked people receiving God's mercy.

> But God demonstrates his own love for us in this: While we were still sinners, Christ died for us. (Romans 5:8)

A picture of warning, repentance and forgiveness. This is the basic theme of the Bible, God bringing salvation to a sinful people.

Second. '...three days and three nights in the heart of the huge fish...'

Why three days and nights in the belly of the fish? God could have used a number of things to change Jonah's direction, so why this way?

When God does something, especially the unusual, He does it for a reason. The three days and nights within the belly is the transition from the old to the new, the dying of one, and the birth of another.

Look at two aspects the story of Jonah represents.

The most obvious one is Jonah's hatred of the Assyrians. (Nineveh was a mighty city within Assyria.) Here Jonah represents man.

The Assyrians were the Israelites' enemy, they were feared, hated and despised. They were becoming a powerful nation and Israel was starting to fall under the shadow of their oppression. Not only did Jonah hate them, but he would also become a traitor to his nation Israel if he brought God's favour upon them. He was not going to budge from the way he felt.

God had to do something extreme for Jonah to comply. Jonah had to die to the way he was thinking and submit to God. This happened while in the belly of the fish. Repentance requires this of us, we have to die to self and our direction and then live for Christ and His will.

> We were therefore buried with him through baptism into death in order that, just as Christ was raised from the dead through the glory of the Father, we too may live a new life. (Romans 6:4)

Once this happened, Jonah went to Nineveh and carried out what God required. But Jonah's resentment continues and is covered in the third reason. The death experience caused a change in direction.

Jesus tells us this death experience is a requirement to follow Him.

> Then he said to them all: 'Whoever wants to be my disciple must deny themselves and take up their cross daily and follow me. For whoever wants to save their life will lose it, but whoever loses their life for me will save it.' (Luke 9:23-24)

A less obvious reason for the three days and nights in the belly is Jonah's representation of the Law. The story of Jonah is the story of the Old Covenant and the New Covenant. There are two aspects of the Law needing to be mentioned here. The first is the Law was limited to only Israel and secondly, the Law could not bring salvation. Because Jonah represented the Law, he could not do what

God asked him to do. The three days in the belly of the whale were essential.

First, the Law was given to the nation of Israel, it was not given for the gentile nations around them, it was given only to Israel. To make this clearer we look at some New Testament examples.

There is a story when Jesus comes into contact with a Gentile woman and responds quite harshly to her request.

> A Canaanite woman from that vicinity came to him, crying out, 'Lord, Son of David, have mercy on me! My daughter is demon-possessed and suffering terribly.' …He answered, 'I was sent only to the lost sheep of Israel.' The woman came and knelt before him. 'Lord, help me!' she said. He replied, 'It is not right to take the children's bread and toss it to the dogs.' (Matthew 15:22, 23-26)

Under the Law, Jesus answered correctly, He understood its limitations, but goes on to demonstrate He is greater than the Law.

We see how restrictive the Law was in Acts 10:9-14,

> About noon the following day as they were on their journey and approaching the city, Peter went up on the roof to pray. He became hungry and wanted something to eat, and while the meal was being prepared, he fell into a trance. He saw heaven opened and something like a large sheet being let down to earth by its four corners. It contained all kinds of four-footed animals, as well as reptiles and birds. Then a voice told him, 'Get up, Peter. Kill and eat.' 'Surely not, Lord!' Peter replied. 'I have never eaten anything impure or unclean.'

Here we see Peter react to that which was unclean and impure. But what was God really referring to here? He wanted Peter to go and preach the Gospel to the Gentiles.

Peter knew the Law:

> He said to them: 'You are well aware that it is against our law for a Jew to associate with or visit a Gentile…' (Acts 10:28a)

Therefore, if God did not show He made it all right to eat unclean or non-kosher[27] foods, Peter would have refused to enter a Gentile's house.

Peter was by no means a scholar of the Law, but he was not willing to break it. Jonah, who represented the Law, could not break it.

The second point concerning the Law is its inability to bring salvation. The Law could only bring temporary relief of sin, but it was never permanent.

> The law is only a shadow of the good things that are coming – not the realities themselves. For this reason it can never, by the same sacrifices repeated endlessly year after year, make perfect those who draw near to worship. Otherwise, would they not have stopped being offered? For the worshippers would have been cleansed once for all, and would no longer have felt guilty for their sins. (Hebrews 10:1-5)

But those are an annual reminder of sins. It's impossible for the blood of bulls and goats to take away sins. Therefore, when Christ came into the world, he said: 'Sacrifices and offerings you did not desire, but a body you prepared for me.'

Only through the death and resurrection of the Lord Jesus Christ did true salvation come to mankind.

The Law concerning both its inability to go outside Israel and

---

27 Kosher – (of food, or premises in which food is sold, cooked, or eaten) satisfying the requirements of Jewish law.

its inability to bring full salvation, needed to die and be replaced by the new.

You can start to understand, Jonah (the Law) could not do what God asked. When God called the Old Covenant to go and preach to the Gentiles, it could not do it. So something had to happen.

The Old Covenant had to die.

> For if there had been nothing wrong with that first covenant, no place would have been sought for another. (Hebrews 8:7)

> The former regulation is set aside because it was weak and useless (for the law made nothing perfect), and a better hope is introduced, by which we draw near to God. (Hebrews 7:18-19)

We will never realise how much Jesus accomplished on and beyond the cross. But from this point, the most monumental change occurred in the history of mankind. One of these changes was the transition between the Old Covenant and the Birth of the New Covenant. The Old Covenant was limited in what it could accomplish, therefore had to die in order for the New Covenant to take effect. Where the Old Covenant centred on the Law, the New Covenant centres on the Lord Jesus Christ.

The Bible reveals little of what happened in the belly of the earth for three days and three nights. Whatever Jesus did, fundamental spiritual dynamics changed. And one of these changes was the Covenants. When Jesus died and rose again the New Covenant was put into effect and now could go into all the world and preach the Gospel.

> He said to them, 'This is what I told you while I was still with you: Everything must be fulfilled that is written about me in the Law of Moses, the Prophets and the Psalms.'

> He opened their minds so they could understand the Scriptures. He told them, 'This is what is written: The Messiah will suffer and rise from the dead on the third day, and repentance for the forgiveness of sins will be preached in his name to all nations, beginning at Jerusalem.' (Luke 24:44-47)

I don't believe Jonah knew he was acting on behalf of the Law, but God used his hatred toward Nineveh to accomplish this analogy.

In the third reason, we see how Jonah's hatred toward the Ninevites is a story in itself.

What did Jesus mean when He said '…and now something greater than Jonah is here'?

Jonah, a prophet of God, was called to go to Nineveh and warn them to repent. Jonah refuses. And when Nineveh repents, Jonah is still angry.

> Jonah began by going a day's journey into the city, proclaiming, 'Forty more days and Nineveh will be overthrown.'
>
> The Ninevites believed God. A fast was proclaimed, and all of them, from the greatest to the least, put on sackcloth. (Jonah 3:4-5)

> When God saw what they did and how they turned from their evil ways, he relented and did not bring on them the destruction he had threatened. (Jonah 3:10)

> But to Jonah this seemed very wrong, and he became angry. (Jonah 4:1)

> 'Now, LORD, take away my life, for it is better for me to die than to live.' (Jonah 4:3)

So why does the Bible go on about Jonah's disobedience and eventual anger? It seems out of place because God's will was accomplished. This was God's will, not Jonah's, so why do we care what Jonah thinks?

The Bible seems to care.

When the story of Jonah is told, this unrelenting anger is never explained. But the Bible screams Jonah's protests in the beginning and the end.

Jonah, a prophet of God, willingly disobeyed God, and when he did obey, was angry with God. Why?

Jonah shows us why Jesus had to bring salvation.

Jonah represents mankind, and God asked him to do something he was incapable of doing. Jonah is an example of how limited the character of man is, and of how the depth of man's love cannot go through with what God requires.

There are two kinds of love represented here – *phileo* love which Jonah was operating in, and *agape* (pronounced – argarpay) love, which God demonstrates. We will come back to these differences.

To see this difference, there is a great passage of scripture pointing this out and that is often misunderstood.

> Love is patient, love is kind. It does not envy, it does not boast, it is not proud. It does not dishonour others, it is not self-seeking, it is not easily angered, it keeps no record of wrongs. Love does not delight in evil but rejoices with the truth. It always protects, always trusts, always hopes, always perseveres. Love never fails. (1 Corinthians 13:4-8a)

When we discuss or think of these verses, this is what we want to, or are encouraged to aspire to. We want to be more like this love.

These verses are not talking about the love of man. As stated earlier, we need to look at the actual words used here. These verses are not talking about man's love, nor wanting to increase man's love. The words used make this clear.

The love in these verses are absolutes, they are perfect. Look how love is described: Love is, love does not, love is not, love always, love never. There is no compromise here, no imperfections. We can never live up to these standards, no matter how virtuous we are. These absolutes can only be accomplished by God.

These verses are not talking about us, they are describing Jesus. The point made here is, our love is limited, our love is not absolute. It is not our love that needs to increase, it is the love of Christ that needs to increase within us.

This story of Jonah simply shows how limited man's love is, compared to God's love. Jonah was acting on his love, not God's. Jonah could not get on the same page as God. Man cannot reach the same heights as God.

> 'As the heavens are higher than the earth, so are my ways higher than your ways and my thoughts than your thoughts.' (Isaiah 55:9)

God had to send His Son Jesus to accomplish what man could not.

Let's return to the Greek words describing love, *phileo* and *agape*. *Phileo* love is the affection or how we feel towards a subject. *Agape* love is seeing a need and putting into action a means to bring about a positive change. John 3:16 is a great example of this.

> For God so loved the world He gave his only begotten Son, that whosoever believeth in him should not perish, but have everlasting life. (KJV)

One of the mistakes we fall into concerning this verse is when we read, 'For God so loved the world.' We read, 'For God so *phileo* the world.'

God did not look down upon the world with great affection, He looked down and saw a rebellious people who rejected Him and were heading for hell. God knew the need and did something about it. 'For God so *agape* the world.'

The love demonstrated here incorporated everything required to reconcile mankind that was separated and under God's wrath, back into His Family. He had to send His only Son. Only God could administer this kind of love to a world that rejected and hated Him. Jonah saw Nineveh as an enemy of Israel that deserved the wrath of God. But God wanted to demonstrate *agape* love, not *phileo* love.

Jonah, a prophet of God, could not in his own ability give forgiveness to his enemy, and this was just one city. Man does not have the ability to love their enemy to the degree the world needed.

God had to send someone greater than man.

'...and now something greater than Jonah is here.' (Matthew 12:41b)

God had to come Himself, in power and favour, as a man - Jesus Christ our Redeemer.

Chapter 12

Changing Water to Wine

> Jesus answered, 'Very truly I tell you, no one can enter the Kingdom of God unless they are born of water and the Spirit.' (John 3:5)

Born of water is the cleansing process needed to be accepted into the Kingdom of God. Water represents the cleansing power, but it all focuses on Christ.

> Have mercy on me, O God, according to your unfailing love; according to your great compassion blot out my transgressions. Wash away all my iniquity and cleanse me from my sin. (Psalm 51:1-2)

It is the blood of Jesus that cleanses us from sin. What has water got to do with blood?

When Jesus walked this earth, one of His first miracles noted by Scripture, was to change water to wine.

> Nearby stood six stone water jars, the kind used by the Jews for ceremonial washing, each holding from twenty to thirty gallons. Jesus said to the servants, 'Fill the jars with water'; so they

filled them to the brim. Then he told them, 'Now draw some out and take it to the master of the banquet.' They did so, and the master of the banquet tasted the water that had been turned into wine... (John 2:6-9a)

Here we see the famous story of the water being changed to wine. This miracle paints a picture of why Jesus Christ came to this earth. The significance of this story is in the type of jars used, the water, the wine and who performed the miracle.

Isn't it a bit odd that He filled not one jar, but others, filling them to the brim, holding from twenty to thirty gallons each? There was enough wine here to send the whole village rolling drunk down its streets. Yet God abhors and detests drunkenness.

> Do not get drunk on wine, which leads to debauchery. Instead, be filled with the Spirit. (Ephesians 5:18)

Practicality would have only required one jar and it wouldn't have needed to be filled to the brim. But Jesus uses all the jars and fills them to the top. This miracle went beyond filling a practical need.

This miracle using these jars demonstrates the difference between ceremonial washing and the cleansing power of Christ. It showed the public these ceremonial practices done under the Law were about to be changed forever through Jesus.

These ceremonial jars represented the way the Law cleansed. It was temporal and not permanent. In this case, it cleaned the outside but not the inside of a man. Even the blood used in sacrifices:

> The blood of goats and bulls and the ashes of a heifer sprinkled on those who are ceremonially unclean sanctify them so that they are outwardly clean. (Hebrews 9:13)

When Jesus changed the water to wine, He had taken something used to cleanse outwardly and changed it into something to be taken internally.

The water used in these jars was for ceremonial washing only. When it was turned to wine, it still represented the same purpose but it now represented what Jesus was going to accomplish through His blood on the cross. The communion we partake of, is the representation of this blood.

Here is the picture emerging from this miracle.

Jesus comes to this earth and fulfils all the requirements of the Law. This is why all the jars are used and are filled to the brim. But the Law could only cleanse temporarily, it couldn't cleanse us sufficiently.

Jesus was substituted for the Law and becomes the sacrifice that cleanses us from sin once and for all. Through the sacrificial blood of Christ, we are cleansed completely from our sins. Christ's sacrificial blood completely satisfied the requirements of God, for the forgiveness of sins.

This miracle says why Jesus came to the earth.

> The blood of goats and bulls and the ashes of heifers sprinkled on those who are ceremonially unclean sanctify them so that they are outwardly clean. How much more, then, will the blood of Christ, who through the eternal Spirit offered himself unblemished to God, cleanse our consciences from acts that lead to death, so that we may serve the living God? For this reason Christ is the mediator of a new covenant, that those who are called may receive the promised eternal inheritance – now that he has died as a ransom to set them free from the sins committed under the first covenant. (Hebrews 9:13-15)

It is also worth taking note this first recorded public miracle was a wedding and one of the final acts concerning this world is the 'Wedding Feast of the Lamb and His Bride.'

> 'Let us rejoice and be glad and give him glory. For the wedding of the Lamb has come, and his bride has made herself ready. Fine linen, bright and clean, was given her to wear.' (Revelation 19:7)

Fine linen stands for the righteous acts of God's holy people.

> Then the angel said to me, 'Write this: Blessed are those who are invited to the wedding supper of the Lamb.' And he added, 'These are the true words of God.' (Revelation 19:8-11)

Chapter 13

Propitiation

> And he is the propitiation for our sins: and not for ours only, but also for the sins of the whole world. (1 John 2:2 KJV)

What Jesus suffered on the cross is barely understood by Christians and in most cases, we take for granted what Jesus accomplished. We know we are saved because of what He did, but do we really comprehend what He had to undergo?

Even in the movie, *The Passion of the Christ*, by Mel Gibson, the physical suffering of Jesus depicted, as brutal as it was, was not enough to pay for the sins of the world. There have been worse physical suffering of Christians throughout history than Christ experienced.

What made the cross of Christ so radically different the sins of the world can now be forgiven through Him? What does it mean, 'He is the propitiation for our sins'?

Jesus had to suffer more than physical punishment, He needed to suffer at the hands of His Heavenly Father.

On the night of His betrayal, we see Jesus, struggling with His Father's will.

> Going a little farther, he fell with his face to the ground and

> prayed, 'My Father, if it is possible, may this cup be taken from me. Yet not as I will, but as you will.' (Matthew 26:39)
>
> 'Abba, Father,' he said, 'everything is possible for you. Take this cup from me. Yet not what I will, but what you will.' (Mark 14:36)
>
> 'Father, if you are willing, take this cup from me; yet not my will, but yours be done.' (Luke 22:42)
>
> Jesus commanded Peter, 'Put your sword away. Shall I not drink the cup the Father has given me?' (John 18:11)

What was in this cup? What made this cup so repulsive to Christ that He asked His Father to take it away?

This cup contained something of the Heavenly Father, Jesus the Eternal Son of God, had never experienced before.

The cup was the full wrath of God. And it was about to be turned toward Him.

Jesus was about to pay in full for our sins (past, present, future).

> Whom God hath set forth to be a propitiation through faith in his blood, to declare his righteousness for the remissions of sins that are past, through the forbearance of God; To declare, I say, at this time his righteousness: that he might be just, and the justifier of him which believeth in Jesus. (Romans 3:25-26 KJV)

The NIV version says it this way:

> God presented Christ as a sacrifice of atonement, through the shedding of His Blood – to be received by faith. He did this to demonstrate His righteousness, because in His forbearance He

> had left the sins committed beforehand unpunished – He did it to demonstrate His righteousness at the present time, so as to be just and the one who justifies those who have faith in Jesus.

Had God left sins beforehand unpunished?

> He will not always accuse, nor will he harbour his anger forever; he does not treat us as our sins deserve or repay us according to our iniquities. (Psalm 103:9-10)

Why not?

God is not a corrupt Judge, therefore He will not allow sins to go unpunished. God's righteousness demands justice and the sentence of sin is death. Yet many of the heroes of the Old Testament committed sins that deserved death. Throughout history, many sins were never met with God's full wrath. Even the blood of animals did not satisfy the requirement of sin.

> It is impossible for the blood of bulls and goats to take away sins. (Hebrews 10:4)

So why did God leave the sins beforehand unpunished?

Because He was going to send His Son, who would bear the full brunt of sin's consequence. God left sins unpunished because His Son was willing to pay in full, what was owed, not only past sins, but present and future. And He now justifies us, through what He endured.

God has been able to show mercy, because of Jesus and what He bore on the cross.

Jesus knew exactly what He was taking on.

> 'Who, being in very nature God, did not consider equality with

God something to be used to his own advantage; rather, he made himself nothing by taking the very nature of a servant, being made in human likeness. And being found in appearance as a man, he humbled himself by becoming obedient to death – even death on a cross. (Philippians 2:6-8)

God made him who had no sin to be sin for us, so that in Him we might become the righteousness of God. (2 Corinthians 5:21)

Upon the cross, Jesus drank down the whole cup of God's wrath.

But God is the judge: he putteth down one, and setteth up another. For in the hand of the LORD there is a cup, and the wine is red; it is full of mixture; and he poureth out of the same: but the dregs therof, all the wicked of the earth shall wring them out, and drink them. (Psalm 75:7-8 KJV)

Jesus drank this cup.

You have put me in the lowest pit, in the darkest depths. Your wrath lies heavily on me; you have overwhelmed me with all your waves. (Psalm 88:6-7)

Why, LORD, do you reject me and hide your face from me? From my youth I have suffered and been close to death; I have borne your terrors and am in despair. Your wrath has swept over me; your terrors have destroyed me. (Psalm 88:14-16)

There are many more descriptions of Christ's suffering on the cross within Scripture, but we will never fully understand the horror and anguish Jesus had to bear. At the height of His anguish and torment, He cried these words: 'My God, My God, why have You forsaken me?' (Matthew 27:46). Jesus experienced the full consequence of man's sin, He faced the total wrath of God.

This propitiation of sin by Christ ripped through the heart of all existence. Jesus had all sin thrust upon Him. It sent shock waves through the angelic host who were poised and waiting for His command. The Father's love was ripped from His hand, replaced by His wrath. He drained every drop of His fury from the cup, upon His Son. The fabric of sin was being torn asunder.

The governing laws were being uprooted. The power of Satan's kingdom was being ripped from his hands and the rights that sin had over mankind, Jesus drew all to Himself. The measure of sin upon Jesus became the measure of His Father's wrath.

Jesus paid the full price for every sin committed, was being committed and all that will be committed. The head of the serpent was being crushed. Jesus was disarming the enemy. When the final drop of God's wrath was spent, Jesus uttered the words, 'It is finished.' He was triumphant:

> And having disarmed the powers and authorities, he made a public spectacle of them, triumphing over them by the cross. (Colossians 2:15)

> Herein is love, not that we loved God, but that He loved us, and sent his Son to be the propitiation for our sins. (1 John 4:10 KJV)

Before Christ took the cross, death could claim us. After He took the cross, death lost its grip upon us. The second we receive what Christ did, we step into eternity with Him.

Part 3

The Tent of Meeting

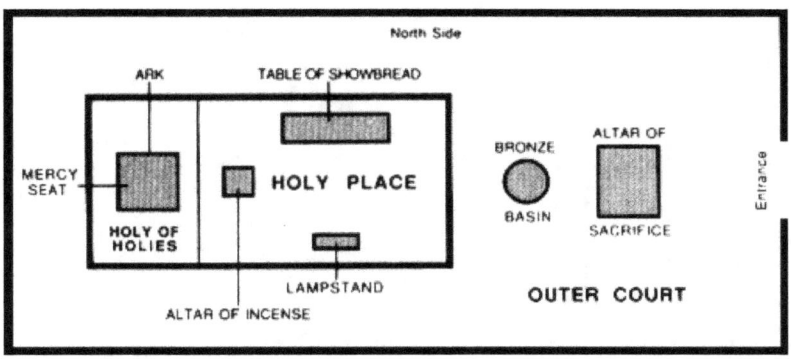

Chapter 14

The Tabernacle – The Tent of Meeting

When we think of Exodus we mainly think about God bringing the Israelites out of Egypt, but a whole lot more happened after that.

God met with Moses on Mount Sinai and gave him the Law. God also gave instructions for the building of the Tabernacle or Tent of Meeting. A big part of Exodus is about this building of the Tabernacle and its holy furnishings. This was important because we see directly the intent of God. To dwell among the people.

The design of the Tabernacle was simple, but significant and deeply profound.

There are three main areas, the Outer Court, the Holy Place and the Holy of Holies. The sacrifices and offerings were done in the outer courts. Only selected Levites could enter the Holy Place. And only the High Priest could enter the Holy of Holies, once a year.

So what relevance is this to us?

Through the Tabernacle, God was showing us He intended us to come into His Presence. Because of our sinful nature, we couldn't just stroll in. The Presence of God accompanying the Israelites in the desert was not some gentle breeze, but a thunderous, terrifying cloud of fire and smoke.

The Israelites understood they couldn't approach God before the Tabernacle was built. This is illustrated when Moses met with God on the Holy Mountain.

> When the people saw the thunder and lightning and heard the trumpet and saw the mountain in smoke, they trembled with fear.
>
> They stayed at a distance and said to Moses, 'Speak to us yourself and we will listen. But do not have God speak to us or we will die.' (Exodus 20:18-19)

They understood their unholy position before a Holy God.

God does something surprising when the Tabernacle is constructed. When He gave instructions for the building of the Tabernacle, He included a material representing man. This material would feature in every part of the Tabernacle, from the Entrance Gate to the Covenant Box in the Holy of Holies.

By using a material representing mankind throughout the Tabernacle, God shows us He was going to make it possible for men and women to come into His Holy Presence.

The Tabernacle was a prophetic picture of God's desire to intimately meet with us.

Even within the Holy of Holies this material is found in one of the holiest of objects, the Covenant Box. God's intention was not to forever dwell in a room where only the High Priest had the right once a year to enter. Through His Son He was going to make it possible for Him to dwell within each one of us, exactly like the Covenant Box.

The prophet Jeremiah writes down the intention of God before it was fulfilled through Christ.

> 'The days are coming,' says the LORD, 'when I will make a new covenant with the people of Israel and with the people of Judah. It will not be like the covenant I made with their ancestors when I took them by the hand to lead them out of Egypt, because they broke my covenant, though I was a husband to them,' says the LORD.

> 'This is the covenant I will make with the people of Israel after that time,' says the LORD. 'I will put my law in their minds and write it on their hearts. I will be their God, and they will be my people. No longer will they teach their neighbour, or say to one another, "Know the LORD," because they will all know me, from the least of them to the greatest,' says the LORD. 'For I will forgive their wickedness and will remember their sins no more.' (Jeremiah 31:31-34)

The Bible says this fulfilment in Hebrews 8:5a,

> They serve at a sanctuary that is a copy and shadow of what is in heaven.

This is why Moses was warned when he was about to build the Tabernacle:

> See to it that you make everything according to the pattern shown you on the mountain.
> But in fact the ministry Jesus has received is as superior to theirs as the covenant of which he is mediator is superior to the old one, since the new covenant is established on better promises.' (Hebrews 8:5b-6; note: Hebrews 8:10-11 quotes Jeremiah 31:31-34)

Here we see the Tabernacle was just a picture of what was to come, that God through the death and resurrection of Jesus, will dwell within us. That is why God chooses to use a material throughout the Tabernacle that represents man.

What was this material, and how could it justifiably be in every part of the Tabernacle, even coming so boldly into the Presence of God?

Acacia wood is found in every part of the Tabernacle.[28] The acacia wood is found in the frame posts of the outer wall right through to the Covenant Box within the Most Holy Place.

But how can the acacia wood be in the Holy Presence of God, if it represents man?

In order for the acacia wood to be able to be present within many parts of the Tabernacle, it could not be openly exposed. (For mankind cannot stand in the Presence of God in their own merit). It needed to be completely covered with the precious metal of gold or bronze. These metals represented Jesus Christ (bronze representing His sacrifice, gold representing His Holiness), who becomes our covering that allows us into the very Throne room of God Almighty.

> So in Christ Jesus you are all children of God through faith, for all of you who were baptised into Christ have clothed yourselves with Christ. (Galatians 3:26-27)

Because Christ went to the cross and bore our sin, he is able to impart His righteousness to us.

> For he hath made him to be sin for us, who knew no sin; that we might be made the righteousness of God in him. (2 Corinthians 5:21 KJV)

We have the righteousness of Christ that gives us the ability to be in the Presence of God.

We come to the understanding we have the ability through Jesus Christ to enter into the very Presence of God. Man is represented

---

28 Acacia wood representing man in the Tabernacle is written about in more detail in this author's book, *Dying to Live*.

throughout the whole of the Tabernacle. From the entrance gate, right through to the Holy of Holies.

One of the reasons only the High Priest entered the Holy of Holies is because this represented you. Understanding the relationship you have with God can only be established between you and God. We as individuals must pursue this, we must establish a relationship that is real. Meeting with God is not only attainable, but necessary.

The building of the Tent of Meeting early on in the journey of the Israelites, was showing us the importance of developing this relationship from the start.

Chapter 15

To Know God

Redemption and salvation are the start of something bigger and greater.

Jesus said you must be born-again.[29] It is just the start, the beginning of the real journey. Salvation opens the door to what God had purposed for us all along, and that is to discover Him.

Paul writes about this in Philippians 3:7-8,

> But whatever were gains to me I now consider loss for the sake of Christ. What is more, I consider everything a loss because of the surpassing worth of knowing Christ Jesus my Lord, for whose sake I have lost all things. I consider them garbage, that I may gain Christ.

To know Christ is now Paul's priority. This is where God wants to take us.

This meeting with and getting to know Christ is the foundation for the rest of our lives.

When we grasp this verse[30] and allow it to penetrate the core of our heart, the same way it transformed Paul, we will connect with

---

29 John 3:3
30 Philippians 3:7-8

the heart of God. Paul understood that to know Christ is the key. When we truly pursue this, we are able to do the will of Him who we will know.

Often we think the main reason Jesus came to this earth was to save man from hell. But that's not the main reason. Jesus came so that we may have eternal life with Him.

> For God so loved the world He gave His only begotten Son, whoever believes in Him should not perish but have everlasting life. (John 3:16 KJV)

Saving us from hell was the start of the reason. The main reason is found in the phrase 'but have everlasting life.'

God's purpose is and always has been for us to come to know Him. The depth of God is infinite, we will only scratch the surface.

To have a better understanding of how infinite the depth of God is, look at the universe we live in. Today's scientists know a great deal about the universe we live in and have some knowledge about the other universes. Yet this knowledge is only one trillionth of what is actually out there. The universe with all its vastness, is still finite, it has a beginning and an end. It is a created realm. You can heat a particle of it to become a gas, or compress it to become a diamond, you can change it, but you cannot cause it to cease to exist. It is finite.

The universe is inside God's Presence. He spoke it into existence. From where did He do this? From an uncreated realm, Alpha and Omega, without beginning or end.

Imagine the universe as a tabletop floating in space, a vibration of existence spoken into being by an uncreated God. There's the universe, any universe, any number of universes, a bunch of tabletops floating in space.

They are finite, each of them. That endless space they are floating in is not. That's His realm, Alpha and Omega. Our purpose is to be reconciled with His realm, without beginning, without end.

On the cross, as He took that cup, Christ saw, experienced, an eternity without His Father, an eternity trapped in a created realm. That's the flesh, the world, the Law, that's hell.

God being infinitely greater than all creation, do we really believe we will figure God out? The knowledge of God we gain on this earth is mind-blowing and fills us to overflowing, yet we are barely scratching the surface of God Almighty.

When Jesus said '…but have everlasting life', this is exactly what He was referring to. To know God is to have abundant life, life in its fullness. And this voyage of discovery will last an eternity.

God's priority for us is to spend time with Him, and get to know Him. God is our reward.

> After this, the word of the LORD came to Abram in a vision: 'Do not be afraid, Abram. I am your shield, your very great reward.' (Genesis 15:1)

In everything we can accomplish in this life, nothing will ever compare to having Christ Jesus revealed to us, for God to open our minds so that we may know Him. This is the highest reward mankind can ever accomplish. King David understood this:

> You, God, are my God, earnestly I seek you; I thirst for you, my whole being longs for you, in a dry and parched land where there is no water. I have seen you in the sanctuary and beheld your power and your glory. Because your love is better than life, my lips will glorify you. I will praise you as long as I live, and in your name I will lift up my hands. I will be fully satisfied as with the richest of foods; with singing lips my mouth will praise you. On my bed I remember you; I think of you through the watches

> of the night. Because you are my help, I sing in the shadow of your wings. I cling to you; your right hand upholds me. (Psalm 63:1-8)

> As the deer pants for streams of water, so my soul pants for you, my God. My soul thirsts for God, for the living God. When can I go and meet with God? (Psalm 42:1-2)

Jesus Himself shows how important it was to spend time with God.

> Jesus did many other things as well. If every one of them were written down, I suppose even the whole world would not have room for the books that would be written. (John 21:25)

Jesus accomplished a huge amount while here on earth, yet not His will but the Father's.

> So Jesus said, 'When you have lifted up the Son of Man, then you will know I am he and I do nothing on my own but speak only what the Father has taught me.' (John 8:28)

Everything Jesus does and says is from His Father. How does He accomplish this?

Jesus made meeting with His Heavenly Father, His priority.

Even at the age of 12, He understood this concept. Luke 2:41-50 tells the story of Jesus' family, relatives and friends going to Jerusalem to celebrate Passover. They left to return home, but Jesus stayed. After three days, Joseph and Mary found Him in the Temple.

> When his parents saw him, they were astonished. His mother said to him, 'Son, why have you treated us like this? Your father and I have been anxiously searching for you.' 'Why were you

searching for me?' he asked. 'Didn't you know I had to be in my Father's house?' But they did not understand what he was saying to them. (Luke 2:48-50)

Jesus knew without a doubt where His priorities lay, even if He was going against His parents understanding.

These are my thoughts concerning the aftermath of this. If Joseph and Mary were good Jewish parents, they probably would have to have disciplined Jesus due to His disobedience because of their misunderstanding. And it probably wasn't a time out. Maybe the Holy Spirit doesn't record this, because Jesus did nothing wrong. It also reminds us we may be punished for doing what God requires.

If there is a desire within to know Christ Jesus with greater intimacy, this is what the Holy Spirit is drawing us into. We don't have to become hermit monks taking a vow of silence living in seclusion for the rest of our lives to accomplish this.

We can come to know God in our everyday lives, it is up to us where we want to put our priorities.

This is the priority of God, and if we ask Him to make it a reality for us and truly mean it, God will go out of His way to make it happen.

In 1994 I prayed that very prayer to God. I said to Him, 'I don't care what You have to do, but I want to know You the way Paul wrote about in Philippians 3:7-8, "…the surpassing worth of knowing Christ Jesus my Lord…"'

A year later, God changed our location, my vocation, my vision and put me in a job that to me was like the back end of a desert. It took me two years to realise God was answering my prayer.

For which I am today, eternally thankful.

God may not have to go to such extremes, but understand this desire is what He wants for all of us and He will work out how this can be established in your life, if you are serious.

Chapter 16

Jesus Christ Our Foundation

> For no one can lay any foundation other than the one already laid, which is Jesus Christ. If anyone builds on this foundation using gold, silver, costly stones, wood, hay or straw, their work will be shown for what it is, because the Day will bring it to light. It will be revealed with fire, and the fire will test the quality of each person's work. (1 Corinthians 3:11-13)

When we allow the above verse to sink in it will permeate our thinking and penetrate our hearts. It's not hard to come to understand that as Christians (born-again, indwelling Spirit) we are now accountable to Christ.

Everything we do from this point on, whether it is of God or not, is built on the foundation of Jesus Christ.

It is vitally important we firmly establish our foundation. Since the foundation is Jesus Christ we need to learn what this means to us.

When we start to truly discover Christ, we have tapped into the eternal belief that sustains us beyond physical, emotional and spiritual needs.

> Then Jesus declared, 'I am the bread of life. Whoever comes to me will never go hungry, and whoever believes in me will never be thirsty.' (John 6:35)

We are now connected to the reason we are alive.

> For in him all things were created: things in heaven and on earth, visible and invisible, whether thrones or powers or rulers or authorities; all things have been created through him and for him. (Colossians 1:16)

We need to resign to the fact anything outside Christ is pointless and not beneficial for us. Christ is our strong fortress:

> But let all who take refuge in you be glad; let them ever sing for joy. Spread your protection over them, that those who love your name may rejoice in you. (Psalm 5:11)

It is Jesus Christ who truly sustains us.

> Do not work for food that spoils, but for food that endures to eternal life, which the Son of Man will give you. For on him God the Father has placed his seal of approval. (John 6:27)

Jesus satisfies a hunger and thirst within us beyond physical nourishment, He satisfies a hunger and thirst only He can satisfy.

If we want direction in our lives, if we want to discover the ultimate truth, if we want to feel truly alive, it is found in Jesus.

> Jesus answered, 'I am the way and the truth and the life. No one comes to the Father except through me.' (John 14:6)

Here we discover our purpose.

> For we are God's handiwork, created in Christ Jesus to do good

works, which God prepared in advance for us to do. (Ephesians 2:10)

Even in tribulations, we have the assurance of Jesus.

> No, in all these things we are more than conquerors through him who loved us. For I am convinced that neither death nor life, neither angels nor demons, neither the present nor the future, nor any powers, neither height nor depth, nor anything else in all creation, will be able to separate us from the love of God that is in Christ Jesus our Lord. (Romans 8:37-39)

We can hand the worries of this world over to Christ.

> 'Come to me, all you who are weary and burdened, and I will give you rest. Take my yoke upon you and learn from me, for I am gentle and humble in heart, and you will find rest for your souls. For my yoke is easy and my burden is light.' (Matthew 11:28-30)

This includes the necessities of life.

> 'Therefore I tell you, do not worry about your life, what you will eat or drink; or about your body, what you will wear. Is not life more than food, and the body more than clothes? Look at the birds of the air; they do not sow or reap or store away in barns, and yet your heavenly Father feeds them. Are you not much more valuable than they? Can any one of you by worrying add a single hour to your life? And why do you worry about clothes? See how the flowers of the field grow. They do not labour or spin. Yet I tell you that not even Solomon in all his splendour

was dressed like one of these. If that is how God clothes the grass of the field, which is here today and tomorrow is thrown into the fire, will he not much more clothe you – you of little faith? So do not worry, saying, "What shall we eat?" or "What shall we drink?" or "What shall we wear?" For the pagans run after all these things, and your heavenly Father knows that you need them. But seek first his kingdom and his righteousness, and all these things will be given to you as well. Therefore do not worry about tomorrow, for tomorrow will worry about itself. Each day has enough trouble of its own.' (Matthew 6:25-34)

The way we conduct ourselves in the world is important.

Each of you should use whatever gift you have received to serve others, as faithful stewards of God's grace in its various forms. If anyone speaks, they should do so as one who speaks the very words of God. If anyone serves, they should do so with the strength God provides, so that in all things God may be praised through Jesus Christ… (1 Peter 4:10-11)

In all aspects of our lives, Jesus Christ is the foundation. The more we know Him, the more the buildings we build will be through Him.

Everything we do on this earth will be tested when we stand before God. You can either try to ignore this fact, or spend time with Christ so the buildings we do build, will not end up in ashes.

Chapter 17

The Holy Spirit – Connecting Us with God

As Christians, meeting with God now becomes the most important aspect of our existence. It must become the foundation of our lives.

But there is a major problem that stands in our way; the flesh.

Operating in the flesh is so deceptive, it can fool us into thinking we are pleasing God. We have the ability to operate in the flesh and convince ourselves it is God. The subject of the flesh will be discussed in greater depth in the next section of this book.

When we meet with God, it cannot be done out of the flesh, but in spirit and truth.

> 'Yet a time is coming and has now come when the true worshippers will worship the Father in the Spirit and in truth, for they are the kind of worshippers the Father seeks. God is spirit, and his worshippers must worship in the Spirit and in truth.' (John 4:23-24)

To truly meet with God, we must be led there by the Holy Spirit.

> 'When the Advocate comes, whom I will send to you from the Father – the Spirit of truth who goes out from the Father – he will testify about me.' (John 15:26)

> 'But when he, the Spirit of truth, comes, he will guide you into all truth. He will not speak on his own; he will speak only what he hears, and he will tell you what is yet to come. He will glorify me because it is from me that he will receive what he will make known to you. All that belongs to the Father is mine. That is why I said the Spirit will receive from me what he will make known to you.' (John 16:13-15)

The Holy Spirit gives us the ability to meet with God. The Holy Spirit cannot be deceived when our desire to meet with God is disingenuous. But it also doesn't mean we have to be spiritually perfect every time we want to meet. It depends on our heart, or desire.

> 'For where your treasure is, there your heart will be also. The eye is the lamp of the body. If your eyes are healthy, your whole body will be full of light.' (Matthew 6:21-22)

When Christ Jesus is the motivation behind all we do, the Holy Spirit is more than willing to reveal Him to us.

This motivation toward Christ rising like a stream of living water from within, is from the Holy Spirit. When we surrender more and more to this the Holy Spirit will reveal Christ more and more.

The purpose of the Holy Spirit is the glorification of Jesus Christ by honouring God the Father.[31] This will come through word, motive and action.

It is for the glorification of Christ Jesus and nothing else that the Spirit supports.

To walk in the Spirit and not the flesh is more than just doing what is right. It is to surrender to Christ Jesus in word, thought, motivation and action.

---

31 Ephesians 1:19-23

We need more of the Holy Spirit in our lives and God encourages this.

> 'So I say to you: Ask and it will be given to you; seek and you will find; knock and the door will be opened to you. For everyone who asks receives; the one who seeks finds; and to one who knocks, the door will be opened. Which of you fathers, if your son asks for a fish, will give him a snake instead? Or if he asks for an egg, will give him a scorpion? If you then, though you are evil, know how to give good gifts to your children, how much more will your Father in heaven give the Holy Spirit to those who ask him!' (Luke 11:9-13)

God promises if we desire the will of Christ Jesus more and more in our lives, He will not give us evil spirits (snakes and scorpions),[32] but the Holy Spirit to accomplish this. It is the Holy Spirit who empowers us to accomplish all that Christ requires. Without the Holy Spirit, we can accomplish nothing.

---

32 Luke 10:19 'I have given you authority to trample on snakes and scorpions and to overcome all the power of the enemy; nothing will harm you.'

Part 4

Learning the Ways of God

Chapter 18

The Spiritual Leviticus Journey

The book of Leviticus is an important book, but it can be difficult to read because of all the rules and regulations, and a lot seem irrelevant to us.

This book is vital because it reveals the desire of God. Leviticus speaks of the Holiness of God and how the Israelites are to conduct themselves before a Holy God. Leviticus teaches the Israelites how to live a Godly life.

This has always been important, because after God set the Israelites free and establishes the Tent of Meeting, He starts to teach them how they should live. This has not changed for us as Christians.

For most Christians, the goal Christ wants for all of us is that we mature in Him.

> So Christ himself gave the apostles, the prophets, the evangelists, the pastors and teachers, to equip his people for works of service, so the body of Christ may be built up until we all reach unity in the faith and in the knowledge of the Son of God and become mature, attaining to the whole measure of the fullness of Christ. Then we will no longer be infants, tossed back and forth by the waves, and blown here and there by every wind of teaching and by the cunning and craftiness of people in their

> deceitful scheming. Instead, speaking the truth in love, we will grow to become in every respect the mature body of him who is the head, that is, Christ. (Ephesians 4:11-15)

This is the desire of Christ for His people and His body (the church). The exceptions are those who are taken soon after salvation. For example, the criminal on the cross beside Jesus (Luke 23:39-43).

In this Leviticus journey I am not suggesting we return to Old Testament law and live by that standard. The process Christians generally undergo is sanctification, where the Holy Spirit teaches us the ways of Christ Jesus and we become more like Him. It is putting our faith into action, the nuts and bolts of our Christianity.

It is discovering what is of God and what isn't, and what it means to live a sacrificial life and walk in that.

> The mind governed by the flesh is death, but the mind governed by the Spirit is life and peace. (Romans 8:6)

> Therefore, I urge you, brothers and sisters, in view of God's mercy, to offer your bodies as a living sacrifice, holy and pleasing to God – this is your true and proper worship. (Romans 12:1)

In the first nine chapters of Leviticus,[33] it talks about the different offerings they brought before the LORD. Whether a Burnt Offering (animal or grain), Fellowship, Unintentional Guilt, Guilt, Ceremonially Unclean (intentionally or unintentionally), Individual Sin or Atonement Offering for the nation.

Every aspect of their lives had a sacrifice. It was an important requirement of God, and they could not just bring it before Him any way they wanted, they had to follow strict guidelines.

---

33 Leviticus 1:2, 2:1, 3:1, 4:2-3, 5:1-6, 6:1-5, 7:1, 8:2, 9:1-7

> Aaron's sons Nadab and Abihu took their censers, put fire in them and added incense; and they offered unauthorised fire before the LORD, contrary to his command. So fire came out from the presence to the LORD and consumed them, and they died before the LORD. (Leviticus 10:1-2)

God required sacrifices and they had to be done His way. What relevance are these sacrifices to us?

As Christians we are called to live a sacrificial life. Even though we don't literally offer sacrifices, living a sacrificial life to God is to become an essential part of our lives. Christ made the ultimate sacrifice and paid the price for our sins.

The sacrificial life we are to live simply means we obey the teachings of Christ.

As Christians, we learn to lay more and more of our lives down for Him.

> Then he said to them all: 'Whoever wants to be my disciple must deny themselves and take up their cross daily and follow me.' (Luke 9:23)

If you have been taught God will fall over Himself to grant you the life you want, you have probably been fed a lie. You may be where you feel truly blessed, but always remember, you are accomplishing His will, not the other way around.

The more we are submitting to Christ, the more we will have the ability to be transformed.

The Leviticus part of our journey is probably the most frustrating and enlightening discoveries we will face in this earthly life. This experience will accompany us all our lives, but it is up to us how much we are willing to surrender to Christ.

This part of our Christian journey can be discovered instantly but take many years to fully understand. While we have breath in our lungs, we have the ability to be transformed more and more to the likeness of Christ. For this to happen, we need to know His ways.

How do we know what is from God and what isn't?

How do we discern between the voice of God, self or the devil?

How do we become living sacrifices, holy and pleasing to God?

You may be disappointed to hear there is no magical formula or seven-step program to achieve the answer. But if we are willing to persevere and endure in the pursuit of God we will grow in the understanding of His truth, and the Holy Spirit will be the Refiner.

This Leviticus journey is learning and discovering Jesus in the seen and unseen. This is the process taking us from being milk suckling babes to mature meat eaters. The sad fact is, many Christians stay milk suckling babes all their lives.

It is true Jesus will take you as you are, but it is not His intention that you remain as you are. The Holy Spirit is not given so we will stay as we are, He is there so we may be transformed.

> Therefore, I urge you, brothers and sisters, in view of God's mercy, to offer your bodies as a living sacrifice, holy and pleasing to God – this is your true and proper worship. Do not conform to the pattern of this world, but be transformed by the renewing of your mind. Then you will be able to test and approve what God's will is – his good, pleasing and perfect will. (Romans 12:1-2)

To achieve this good, pleasing and perfect will, we must be prepared to take up the cross daily and follow Christ. The Spirit will bring opportunities if we are willing to be transformed by Him.

These transforming processes will take many different forms. From outside challenges to inward struggles, from the gleaning of others to personal enlightenment. From the Word of God, the reality of prayer, the gifts and fruits of the Spirit.

From the edification and encouragement of other believers, the helping and being helped in need. There are many more, but whatever the journey, it will be uniquely designed by the Holy Spirit for you.

Knowing the Bible is one of the ways to achieve this. Learning to consistently read the whole Bible on a regular basis, will equip us with God's ways. When we become familiar with God's Word, we become familiar with His Way.

God doesn't want everyone to become scholars of His Word, but He does want us to know His truths and principles. When we read the Word, the Holy Spirit will teach us. If we seriously want to honour God, this must become one of our disciplines. The Holy Spirit loves revealing the truths of Christ within its pages.[34]

Situations will always arise in our lives bringing some level of discomfort. When dealing with humans, sooner or later, they will irritate, annoy, make you furious, misunderstand, grate you the wrong way, hurt and insult.

God allows these things to happen, so we respond His way, rather than defaulting back to the pattern of this world. Learning to be sensitive to the leading of the Spirit comes through continual obedience.

The Holy Spirit does not have a set way of responding, attached to specific afflictions. Whatever way the Spirit leads, it will always line up with the Word of God.

For all born-again believers, a battle now rages within. And this

---

34 A reading hint: If you want to become familiar with the Bible but don't know where to start, just pick a book and read it, at least one chapter a day. Do this consistently switching between Old and New Testament and ask the Holy Spirit to help.

battle depends on how we respond; whether in accordance with the Spirit, or the flesh.

> So I say, walk by the Spirit, and you will not gratify the desires of the flesh. For the flesh desires what is contrary to the Spirit, and the Spirit what is contrary to the flesh. They are in conflict with each other, so that you are not to do whatever you want. (Galatians 5:16-17)

Galatians 5:22-23 gives us the tools to apply to every situation we may face with others:

> …love, joy, peace, patience, kindness, goodness, gentleness, faithfulness and self-control. Against these there is no law.

These fruits of the Spirit are supernaturally empowered and imparted into our lives by the Holy Spirit. If we respond with either or any of these to people who vex us, the evil one has no reply because 'against these there is no Law'.

It is interesting self-control comes last on the list, given it is usually the first fruit we need to apply before we can use any of the others.

Jesus said in John 6:63,

> 'The Spirit gives life; the flesh counts for nothing. The words I have spoken to you – they are full of the Spirit and life.'

Again in Romans 8:12-13,

> Therefore, brothers and sisters, we have an obligation – but it is not to the flesh, to live according to it. For if you live according

to the flesh, you will die; but if by the Spirit you put to death the misdeeds of the body, you will live.

There are many more ways in which we have the opportunity to be sanctified, but the result is always the same – to be transformed to the likeness of the Lord Jesus Christ.

Chapter 19

A Duel/Dual to the Death

The book of Romans is an excellent microcosm of the whole of the Gospel, from the hopelessness of mankind to the successful and victorious life in Christ Jesus.[35]

Romans makes clear the position of mankind compared to the position of the Holy Almighty God. It tells us how this impossible gap is bridged and how to maintain a successful life through obedience to the Father, Son and the Holy Spirit.

Chapter 7 of Romans is a pivotal chapter because it explains why we have this continual battle with sin even though we are new creations under the Lordship of Christ, with the indwelling of the Holy Spirit.

Before we look at chapter seven more closely, we need to establish how God brings mankind to Himself against impossible odds. And how He equips us to be victorious against impossible odds.

The first three chapters of Romans says emphatically how mankind, Jew and Gentile, have all sinned and fallen short of the glory of God.

In chapter 1, Romans first addresses the condition of all mankind.

---

35 This chapter is so important, it is also included in my book, *To Be a Five Talent Servant*. I am also writing a book on this subject.

> For since the creation of the world God's invisible qualities – his eternal power and divine nature – have been clearly seen, being understood from what has been made, so that people are without excuse. For although they knew God, they neither glorified him as God nor gave thanks to him, but their thinking became futile and their foolish hearts were darkened. (Romans 1:20-21)

Because mankind deliberately rejected God, He gave them over to deception which blinded them.

The Jews considered themselves separate from this debauchery and safe because they were descendants of Abraham and had the Law of Moses. They did not bow down to detestable idols like the pagan Gentiles.

But Paul makes it clear they are in the same predicament as the Gentiles.

Romans says the Jews were unable to obey the righteous requirements of the Law in their own strength.

> You who boast in the law, do you dishonour God by breaking the law? As it is written: 'God's name is blasphemed among the Gentiles because of you.' (Romans 2:23-24)

The Jews failed miserably because they tried to obey God in their own strength, which made them disconnected to God. Because of this, the Jews had also rejected God just like the Gentiles.

The Bible says Jews and Gentiles operating in their own strength cannot obey God.

> What shall we conclude then? Do we have any advantage? Not at all. For we have already made the charge that Jews and Gentiles alike are all under the power of sin. As it is written: 'There is no one righteous, not even one; there is no one who understands;

there is no one who seeks God. All have turned away, they have together become worthless; there is no one who does good, not even one.' (Romans 3:9-12)

The next two chapters bring the answer to this dire situation for mankind.

It is through faith that righteousness is imparted to us. Romans chapter 4 clearly shows it has always been through faith and that pleases God.

We need to understand clearly what Biblical faith is. Faith must include both God and man. Faith is believing and obeying the instruction of the Holy Spirit.

> And without faith it is impossible to please God, because anyone who comes to him must believe that he exists and that he rewards those who earnestly seek him. (Hebrews 11:6)

Faith is believing God above everything else. It is by faith and not by our works that we are brought closer to God (Romans 4:2-3). If Abraham was justified by works, he had something to boast about – but not before God. What does Scripture say? 'Abraham believed God, and it was credited to him as righteousness.'

> Therefore, the promise comes by faith, so that it may be by grace and may be guaranteed to all Abraham's offspring – not only to those who are of the law but also to those who have the faith of Abraham. He is the father of us all. (Romans 4:16)

Romans chapter 5 says it is says faith in Jesus Christ that now imparts God's righteousness.

> Therefore, since we have been justified through faith, we have

> peace with God through our Lord Jesus Christ, through whom we have gained access by faith into this grace in which we now stand. And we boast in the hope of the glory of God. (Romans 5:1-2)

We are put right before God through Jesus Christ.

> But God demonstrates his own love for us in this: While we were still sinners, Christ died for us. Since we have now been justified by his blood, how much more shall we be saved from God's wrath through him! (Romans 5:8-9)

It is through faith alone we are justified before God and are welcomed into His family.

Now that we are accepted, the Bible says a radical new reality for us which we may find hard to believe. Romans chapter 6 clearly tells us the results of our faith in Christ. If we truly believe Scripture, this chapter and many others throughout the Bible make some startling statements.

It says as born-again, new creations, we are no longer subject to sin.

> We are those who have died to sin; how can we live in it any longer? (Romans 6:2)

When Jesus died on the cross, He conquered sin once and for all. He conquered death itself.

When we are born-again we experience the same.

> Or don't you know that all of us who were baptised into Christ Jesus were baptised into his death? We were therefore buried with him through baptism into death in order that, just as

Christ was raised from the dead through the glory of the Father, we too may live a new life. For if we have been united with him in a death like his, we will certainly also be united with him in a resurrection like his. For we know that our old self was crucified with him so that the body ruled by sin might be done away with, that we should no longer be slaves to sin – because anyone who has died has been set free from sin. (Romans 6:3-7)

The Bible says we no longer sin because we are now in Christ Jesus who has conquered sin and does not submit to it.

Do we believe this? This point is made clear again in Romans 6:10-11,

The death he died, he died to sin once for all; but the life he lives, he lives to God. In the same way, count yourselves dead to sin but alive to God in Christ Jesus.

Do we really understand what the Bible is saying? That we no longer have to submit to sin because we are already victorious in Christ.

The Bible emphasises this point.

But thanks be to God that, though you used to be slaves to sin, you have come to obey from your heart the pattern of teaching that has now claimed your allegiance. You have been set free from sin and have become slaves to righteousness. (Romans 6:17-18)

Are we slaves to righteousness? The answer is probably, no. Who is wrong here, the Bible or us? Is the Bible wrong or is it our understanding of what it means to be a Christian that is faulty?

Is the Bible saying that Christians no longer have to sin, or is it saying Christians no longer sin?

The Bible is saying Christians no longer sin. But I still sin, and I know I am a Christian. We need to ask ourselves, do we truly believe Scripture?

Now take Romans 6:3-7, especially 6:5,

> For if we have been united with him in a death like his, we will certainly also be united with him in a resurrection like his.

When we become born-again believers with the indwelling of the Holy Spirit, we are told we are united to Christ. If we are united to Christ and Christ is united to us, how can we sin? If we have been crucified with Christ, then sin has been crucified in us. Our old self who was a slave to sin has been crucified and killed.

The Christian identity is found in the new creation.

> Therefore, if anyone is in Christ, the new creation has come: The old has gone, the new is here! (2 Corinthians 5:17)

Our new creation pledges its allegiance to God through Christ Jesus. This is our true identity, we are new creations, united in Christ. Our old Adamic man has been crucified, but we have also been resurrected in Christ. This means we have conquered sin.

Is the Bible suggesting that Christians do not sin?

No, it's not suggesting, it's saying we don't. Let's look at some other scriptures confirming this.

> So I say, walk by the Spirit, and you will not gratify the desires of the flesh. (Galatians 5:16)

You will not. That's a declaration, not a suggestion.

> We know anyone born of God does not continue to sin. The

> One who was born of God keeps them safe, and the evil one cannot harm them. (1 John 5:18)

The born-again Christian does not continue to sin.

> No one who is born of God will continue to sin, because God's seed remains in them; they cannot go on sinning, because they have been born of God. (1 John 3:9)

> As obedient children, do not conform to the evil desires you had when you lived in ignorance. But just as he who called you is holy, so be holy in all you do; for it is written: 'Be holy, because I am holy.' (1 Peter 1:14-16)

> But if anyone obeys his word, love for God is truly made complete in them. This is how we know we are in him: Whoever claims to live in him must live as Jesus did. (1 John 2:5-6)

As stated earlier, this is probably not our reality, because we continue to sin. So how can these Scriptural statements boldly claim Christians do not sin?

Romans chapter 7 brings the answer to this painful predicament.

This next passage of Scripture has produced provocative debates and no one seems to agree who this wretched man is. I truly believe if we understand who this man is, then the rest of Scripture starts to make a whole lot of sense.

This next passage is quite long and to understand how Scripture can make such bold statements about our position as Christians, we need to view it more closely.

> Was then that which is good made death unto me? God forbid. But sin, that it might appear sin, working death in me by that

which is good; that sin by the commandment might become exceeding sinful. For we know the law is spiritual: but I am carnal, sold under sin. For that which I do I allow not: for what I would, that do I not; but what I hate, that do I. If then I do that which I would not, I consent unto the law that it is good. Now then it is no more I that do it, but sin that dwelleth in me. For I know that in me (that is, in my flesh,) dwelleth no good thing: for to will is present with me; but how to perform that which is good I find not.

For the good that I would I do not: but the evil which I would not, that I do. Now if I do that I would not, it is no more I that do it, but sin that dwelleth in me. I find then a law, that, when I would do good, evil is present with me. For I delight in the law of God after the inward man: But I see another law in my members, warring against the law of my mind, and bringing me into captivity to the law of sin which is in my members. O wretched man that I am! Who shall deliver me from the body of this death? (Romans 7:13-24 KJV)[36]

Before we establish who this 'wretched man' is, we need to establish who he is not. Is he a non-Christian? No.

Romans 3:10-13 says there is no one who understands and there is no one who seeks God, both Jew and Gentile. These verses say a non-Christian working out things in their own strength, is blind to the righteous requirements of God's law. But these passages are saying this man has been spiritually awakened.

For we know that the law is spiritual... (Romans 7:14)

---

[36] Out of all the English versions, the King James Version is the most accurate concerning this passage of Scripture.

> For the good that I would I do not... (Romans 7:19)
>
> For I delight in the law of God after the inward man. (Romans 7:22)
>
> Wherefore the law is holy, and the commandment holy, and just, and good. (Romans 7:12)

This can't be a non-Christian because this understanding and these inward desires to please God have been spiritually awakened.

> For I was alive without the law once: but when the commandment came... (Romans 7:9)

God's righteous requirements can only be fully understood when we have been spiritually awakened.
This 'wretched man' has been spiritually awakened, therefore it can't be a non-Christian. Is he a Christian? No.

> For sin, taking occasion by the commandment, deceived me, and by it slew me. (Romans 7:11)
>
> If then I do that which I would not, I consent unto the law that it is good. (Romans 7:16)

This point needs to be made clear concerning the commandment and the law written about here. These are the righteous commandments or the righteous law God requires and are only understood by those who belong to Him.
This is Paul writing about himself and it is generally known Paul was an expert in the Law, before he became a Christian. So how can he write about himself in Romans 7:9,

> For I was alive without the law once: but when the commandment came, sin revived, and I died.

How can Paul say, 'For I was alive without the law once...?'

When he obeyed the Law previously, he obeyed it by man's standard, not God's. For example, if they didn't actually commit adultery, they obeyed the Law.

But Jesus shone true light on what the commandment required.

> 'You have heard that it was said, "You shall not commit adultery." But I tell you that anyone who looks at a woman lustfully has already committed adultery with her in his heart.' (Matthew 5:27-28)

This is one of the sins Paul had failed in:

> What shall we say? Is the law sin? God forbid. Nay, I had not known sin, but by the law: for I had not known lust, except the law had said, Thou shalt not covet. (Romans 7:7)

Covet here means wrongfully desire after. Therefore, it is the Spirit that highlights the requirements of the Law, and it is only through the Spirit we can obey this law.

Getting back to this 'wretched man', the verses within this passage of Romans clearly tell us this is not a Christian because he is sold under sin, and the Bible clearly tells us we are not sold under sin.

> You have been set free from sin and have become slaves to righteousness. (Romans 6:18)

If this 'wretched man' is not a non-Christian and he is not a Christian, then who is he?

Within the passages of Romans 7:13-24 the answer is given.

> For we know that the law is spiritual: but I am carnal, sold under sin. (Romans 7:14)

> For I know that in me (that is, in my flesh,) dwelleth no good thing... (Romans 7:18)

The 'wretched man' is our carnal nature, or our fleshy worldly nature, or our self that operates outside of Christ.

When we become Christians, we are new creations,[37] born-again,[38] children of God.[39] As Christians we are in Christ. Therefore, we are connected to His death and resurrection.

Christians are victorious (because of what Christ has accomplished). Christians no longer sin (because of what Christ has accomplished). But Christians still live in a corruptible, perishable body. Sin still lies dormant within this body. This nature of ours is known as the 'carnal nature' or the 'flesh'. Or it is when we operate in our own strength, not submitted to Christ.

Jesus addresses this in Luke 9:23.

> Then he said to them all: 'Whoever wants to be my disciple must deny themselves and take up their cross daily and follow me.'

Jesus is telling all those who follow Him to put something to death every day. What is Jesus telling us to kill every day? Our carnal fleshy nature.

---

[37] 2 Corinthians 5:17, Galatians 6:15
[38] John 3:3, 3:7, 1 Peter 1:23
[39] John 1:12, Romans 8:14, Galatians 3:26, 1 John 3:1-2, 3:10, 5:2, 5:19

Why do we need to kill this every day? Because our carnal fleshy nature doesn't submit to Christ.

The following scripture is quite long but it makes it clear this fleshy carnal nature does not belong to our Christian life.

> There is therefore now no condemnation to them which are in Christ Jesus, who walk not after the flesh, but after the Spirit. For the law of the Spirit of life in Christ Jesus has made me free from the law of sin and death.
>
> For what the law was powerless to do because it was weakened by the flesh, God did by sending his own Son in the likeness of sinful flesh to be a sin offering. And so he condemned sin in the flesh, in order that the righteous requirement of the law might be fully met in us, who do not live according to the flesh but according to the Spirit.
>
> Those who live according to the flesh have their minds set on what the flesh desires; but those who live in accordance with the Spirit have their minds set on what the Spirit desires. The mind governed by the flesh is death, but the mind governed by the Spirit is life and peace. The mind governed by the flesh is hostile to God; it does not submit to God's law, nor can it do so. Those who are in the realm of the flesh cannot please God.
>
> You, however, are not in the realm of the flesh but are in the realm of the Spirit, if indeed the Spirit of God lives in you. And if anyone does not have the Spirit of Christ, they do not belong to Christ. But if Christ is in you, then even though your body is subject to death because of sin, the Spirit gives life because of righteousness. And if the Spirit of him who raised Jesus from the dead is living in you, he who raised Christ from the dead will also give life to your mortal bodies because of his Spirit who lives in you.

> Therefore, brothers and sisters, we have an obligation – but it is not to the flesh, to live according to it. For if you live according to the flesh, you will die; but if by the Spirit you put to death the misdeeds of the body, you will live. For those who are led by the Spirit of God are the children of God. The Spirit you received does not make you slaves, so that you live in fear again; rather, the Spirit you received brought about your adoption to sonship. And by him we cry, 'Abba, Father'. (Romans 8:1-15 KJV & NIV)

Romans 7 tells us what wretched men and women we are when we operate in our carnal fleshy nature.

> What a wretched man I am. Who will rescue me from this body that is subject to death? (Romans 7:24)

> Thanks be to God, who delivers me through Jesus Christ our Lord. So then, I myself in my mind am a slave to God's law, but in my sinful nature a slave to the law of sin. (Romans 7:25)

Romans chapter 8 tells us how we can deal with this carnal fleshy nature.

As Christians, there is a dual battle that will continue to rage within us until we meet Christ face to face and are transformed from the corruptible to the incorruptible, from the perishable to the imperishable.[40] Until then, as Christians, there will always be warfare of the Spirit against the flesh, because our carnal fleshy nature wars against the Spirit. It is a duel to the death.

This point is very important to understand, our carnal fleshy nature is not Christian. The Bible emphatically says this.

---

40 1 Corinthians 15:52-54

> The mind governed by the flesh is death, but the mind governed by the Spirit is life and peace. The mind governed by the flesh is hostile to God; it does not submit to God's law, nor can it do so. Those who are in the realm of the flesh cannot please God. (Romans 8:6-8)

When we operate in our carnal fleshy nature, we are hostile to God, we cannot submit to God's will and operating in the flesh leads to death. For all who have accepted Jesus Christ as Lord of their lives, there are now two natures within us: our born-again regenerated nature which is Spirit-led and our carnal fleshy nature which gives rise to sin and lies dormant within the members of our body.

With an understanding of this dual battle, all the scriptures concerning carnal flesh and the Spirit now make sense.

We have already seen some examples from Romans, here are some other examples.

> 'Watch and pray so that you will not fall into temptation. The spirit is willing, but the flesh is weak.' (Matthew 26:41)

> So I say, walk by the Spirit, and you will not gratify the desires of the flesh. For the flesh desires what is contrary to the Spirit, and the Spirit what is contrary to the flesh. They are in conflict with each other, so that you are not to do whatever you want. (Galatians 5:16-17)

> Those who belong to Christ Jesus have crucified the flesh with its passions and desires. Since we live by the Spirit, let us keep in step with the Spirit. (Galatians 5:24-25)

The Apostle Paul recognised this conflict and wrote about it often; this is just one example:

> Do you not know in a race all the runners run, but only one gets the prize? Run in such a way as to get the prize. Everyone who competes in the games goes into strict training. They do it to get a crown that will not last, but we do it to get a crown that will last forever.
>
> Therefore I do not run like someone running aimlessly; I do not fight like a boxer beating the air. No, I strike a blow to my body and make it my slave so that after I have preached to others, I myself will not be disqualified for the prize. (1 Corinthians 9:24-27)

Paul knew this battle well; he tried to fight it in his own strength and failed miserably. He learnt that the battle is already won in Christ Jesus and that walking in the Spirit is the only answer; but first we must put the flesh to death.

It is important to note this chapter isn't trying to say we must live sinless, perfect lives. That's guaranteed to fail. This chapter is to let us know the reality of what we face within ourselves.

As Christians, there are now two paths we can choose, the spiritual or the carnal, it is that simple.

But here is the reality, if we are not continually pursuing Christ, our carnal nature will prevail. That is why Jesus said, 'Take up your cross daily and follow me.'

It should not be seen as an onerous task. Everything done in His strength is done in joy and in peace, a deeper and far more powerful 'pleasure' than anything the flesh can offer. The flesh gradually diminishes and the pleasure, the peace in Him, increases.

Releasing His strength into our lives ensures we will overcome. He does it for us.

Chapter 20

The Tree of Knowledge Versus the True Vine

The previous chapter discussed the dual battle that goes on within concerning the carnal flesh and the Spirit.

This chapter looks at the origins of this battle and why, we as Christians need to understand why our carnal fleshy nature is so pervasive in our lives. The previous chapter showed the two different natures within Christians, the carnal and the spiritual.

This chapter will look into the source of these two natures. Or, what feeds our carnal nature and what feeds our spiritual nature.

There are two types of fruit in this world that will feed us. One comes from the Tree of Knowledge and the other comes from the True Vine. One is from the devil and the other is from the Lord Jesus Christ.

There are only two types of fruit we can produce, good fruit or bad fruit. The Tree of Knowledge can only produce bad fruit and the True Vine can only produce good fruit.

> 'Enter through the narrow gate. For wide is the gate and broad is the road that leads to destruction, and many enter through it. But small is the gate and narrow the road that leads to life, and only a few find it.
>
> 'By their fruit you will recognise them. Do people pick grapes from thornbushes, or figs from thistles? Likewise, every good

tree bears good fruit, but a bad tree bears bad fruit. A good tree cannot bear bad fruit, and a bad tree cannot bear good fruit.' (Matthew 7:13-14, 16-18)

The narrow gate and narrow path is Jesus Christ, the wide gate and broad road is everything done outside of Christ. The good tree is Jesus Christ and the bad tree is the pattern of this world. The good tree is the True Vine.

'I am the true vine, and my Father is the gardener.' (John 15:1)

The bad tree is the Tree of Knowledge and wide is its gate and broad is its road. All those outside of Christ, belong to this tree regardless of awareness. This tree operates independently of Christ, it does not submit to the Lord.

Christians have the ability to get their sustenance from the True Vine. Christians also have got the ability to go back to the Tree of Knowledge, or the carnal fleshy nature. Therefore, we (Christians) have got the ability to produce good and bad fruit. We can only produce two types of fruit in this world, good or bad.

Before we carry on I need to clarify a misunderstanding that may come from Matthew 7:19 ('Every tree that does not bear good fruit is cut down and thrown into the fire'). All Christians have the True Vine, this means we have Jesus Christ, who can only produce good fruit.

God cannot cut this tree down. All those outside of Christ and even those who think they are Christians, but are not, belong to the Tree of Knowledge, producing only bad fruit. This tree God will cut down and throw into the fire. As long as the Holy Spirit dwells within us, we will not be thrown into the fires of hell, only the things we do outside of Christ will be burnt up.

> If what has been built survives, the builder will receive a reward. If it is burned up, the builder will suffer loss but yet will be saved – even though only as one escaping the flames. (1 Corinthians 3:14-15)

We are warned if we are continually consuming bad fruit this will affect us and even though God is longsuffering, He warns that giving in to our carnal fleshy nature leads to death (Romans 8:6, 8:13). It also makes the point that when we give in to the carnal nature, we are dead to our spiritual nature and vice-versa.

The ability to produce good and bad fruit is mentioned in 1 Corinthians 3:11-13,

> For no one can lay any foundation other than the one already laid, which is Jesus Christ. If anyone builds on this foundation using gold, silver, costly stones, wood, hay or straw, their work will be shown for what it is, because the Day will bring it to light. It will be revealed with fire, and the fire will test the quality of each person's work.

This verse alone should be enough to make this next statement a reality for us, '…continue to work out your salvation with fear and trembling' (Philippians 2:12b).

God makes it clear it matters what tree we are producing fruit from:

> The mind governed by the flesh is hostile to God; it does not submit to God's law, nor can it do so. Those who are in the realm of the flesh cannot please God. You, however, are not in the realm of the flesh but are in the Spirit, if indeed the Spirit of God lives in you. And if anyone does not have the Spirit of

> Christ, they do not belong to Christ. But if Christ is in you, then even though your body is subject to death because of sin, the Spirit gives life because of righteousness. Therefore, brothers and sisters, we have an obligation – but it is not to the flesh, to live according to it. (Romans 8:7-12)

The question now needs to be asked: Are we aware when we are operating under the influence of the Tree of Knowledge, the source of our carnal nature?

The pattern of this world is subtle and can mimic godly living, deceiving us into thinking we are pleasing God. Eve was not deceived by the evil of the fruit, but the alluring good.

> When the woman saw that the fruit of the tree was good for food and pleasing to the eye, and also desirable for gaining wisdom, she took some and ate it. She also gave some to her husband, who was with her, and he ate it. (Genesis 3:6)

The deception of this tree for most Christians is not the blatant evil, but the deceiving good.

How often do we believe we are responding justifiably before God, when we are walking in the pattern of this world.

> Do not conform to the pattern of this world, but be transformed by the renewing of your mind… (Romans 12:2)

To get a better understanding how deceptive this Tree of Knowledge is, we need to see what Jesus says about it.

> 'If anyone comes to me and does not hate father and mother, wife and children, brothers and sisters – yes, even their own life – such a person cannot be my disciple. And whoever does not

carry their cross and follow me cannot be my disciple.' (Luke 14:26-27)

This verse has always been problematic for interpretation because it sounds contradictory to Scripture and offensive to our common sense. So usually, the word hate is replaced with, 'love Christ more than'.

The original Greek text specifically uses the word *miseo*,[41] which means to hate, pursue with hatred, detest, to be hated, detested. So what is Christ referring to here?

Jesus points out two facts – the pattern of this world and how to overcome it. The reason Christ uses the word hate against the ones we love (father, mother, wife, children, brother, sister, self), is because the pattern of this world has the ability to permeate everything.

Everything we know and do is a product of the Tree of Knowledge, if it hasn't come under the submission of Christ. Therefore, the way we think, respond, act, react, and so on, can all be fruit from the Tree of Knowledge.

Even the good that we think is pleasing to God, can be a product of the Tree of Knowledge. This tree permeates every aspect of our lives whether we want it to or not. This tree can only produce bad fruit and if we are operating under its influence we are not submitted to Christ.

We are to follow the teachings of Jesus Christ and not those who are close to us if they are connected to the Tree of Knowledge. We are not to treat them disrespectfully.

You can still live in harmony with your loved ones if your relationship with Christ is not compromised by them. Our allegiance is to Jesus the Messiah and no one else. When we do this, the Holy

---

41 *Strong's Concordance* G3404

Spirit is able to impart wisdom that will give us exactly what we need for that particular moment or circumstance.

Once we understand this concept of good and bad fruit, we can identify with the Apostle Paul when confronted with this relentless attack.

> What a wretched man I am. Who will rescue me from this body that is subject to death? (Romans 7:24)

God did not leave us to wallow in this despair, He gave us an answer.

> Thanks be to God, who delivers me through Jesus Christ our Lord! So then, I myself in my mind am a slave to God's law, but in my sinful nature a slave to the law of sin. (Romans 7:25)

The Bible makes plain we will continue to struggle with our sinful nature until we die. The answer can only come when we are willing to obey Luke 9:23,

> Then he said to them all: 'Whoever wants to be my disciple must deny themselves and take up their cross daily and follow me.'

The sinful nature is poison within our bodies and this poison will influence us if we're not surrendering our lives to Christ. The only way to counter this poison, is to take up our cross daily so that we may be transformed by the Spirit.

The Tent of Meeting experience we develop with our Lord becomes such a vital part of our lives. It is the only way we can truly overcome the influence of the Tree of Knowledge. This battle we have with our sinful nature and walking in the Spirit is portrayed repeatedly throughout Scripture.

The Bible doesn't treat us like victims, where we have no control over the influence of the Tree of Knowledge.

> When tempted, no one should say, 'God is tempting me.' For God cannot be tempted by evil, nor does he tempt anyone; but each person is tempted when they are dragged away by their own evil desire and enticed.
>
> After desire has conceived, it gives birth to sin; and sin, when it is full-grown, gives birth to death. Don't be deceived, my dear brothers and sisters. Every good and perfect gift is from above, coming down from the Father of the heavenly lights, who does not change like shifting shadows. (James 1:13-17)

Following the pattern of this world, which comes from the Tree of Knowledge, falls into this category. We have a responsibility now to abide in the True Vine. When we try to conquer sin in our own strength we will fail, because sin can only be truly conquered through Christ.

If you think God is deliberately trying to get us to realise we are hopelessly pathetic when it comes to obeying His will, you would be right. It is only in this sense of hopelessness in trusting our own ability, do we come to a place of surrender.

> 'Blessed are the poor in spirit, for theirs is the kingdom of heaven.' (Matthew 5:3)

When we realise our hopelessness and surrender to Christ, the Spirit takes over.

> Therefore, my dear friends, as you have always obeyed – not only in my presence, but now much more in my absence – continue to work out your salvation with fear and trembling, for it

is God who works in you to will and to act in order to fulfil his good purpose. (Philippians 2:12-13)

When we surrender to the True Vine, it's God's strength maintaining us, not our strength.

Jesus reinforces this in Matthew 7:24-25,

'Therefore everyone who hears these words of mine and puts them into practice is like a wise man who built his house on the rock. The rain came down, the streams rose, and the winds blew and beat against that house; yet it did not fall, because it had its foundation on the rock.'

There are only two types of fruit we can produce on this earth, good or bad, the carnal or the Spirit. Christ has given us the ability to choose.

Chapter 21

Obedience

> In fact, though by this time you ought to be teachers, you need someone to teach you the elementary truths of God's word all over again. You need milk, not solid food! Anyone who lives on milk, being still an infant, is not acquainted with the teaching about righteousness. But solid food is for the mature, who by constant use have trained themselves to distinguish good from evil. (Hebrews 5:12-14)

Walking in obedience is a sign of maturity within a Christian, especially when no one else is observing you. Obedience is the fruit that should be produced within all Christians. The Bible puts it this way:

'Produce fruit in keeping with repentance.' (Matthew 3:8)

When we love the Lord and willingly spend time with Him the desire grows and we want to be more obedient.

> And this is my prayer: that your love may abound more and more in knowledge and depth of insight, so that you may be able to discern what is best and may be pure and blameless for the day of Christ, filled with the fruit of righteousness that

comes through Jesus Christ – to the glory and praise of God. (Philippians 1:9-11)

Either disobedience or lack of love produces a conundrum keeping us in an immature state, or on the outer circles of God's love. No matter how much you love the Lord, your heart may even be overflowing with love for God, but if you are not being obedient in areas that God has drawn attention to, then you will remain in a fickle relationship. This produces inconsistencies keeping us in the outer courts of God's Presence.

If you are trying to live a righteous life, but spend very little or no quality time with the Lord your righteous living will be accomplished in your own strength, which again, produces a shallow relationship with God.

Spiritual maturity requires both love for Christ and obedience working together. The Bible says in James 2:26,

> For as the body without the spirit is dead, so faith without works is dead also. (KJV)

Jesus puts it more poignantly in John 14:23,

> Jesus replied, 'Anyone who loves me will obey my teaching, My Father will love them, and we will come to them and make our home with them.'

It pleases Christ when we love Him with all our heart and are walking obediently before Him with our soul, mind and strength.

Now here is another factor needing serious consideration. Many people who call themselves Christian, are not Christian. Paul tells the Corinthians to test whether they are Christian.

> Examine yourselves to see whether you are in the faith; test yourselves. Do you not realise that Christ Jesus is in you – unless, of course, you fail the test? (2 Corinthians 13:5)

So how do you test yourself whether you are in the faith? I can't give you a list of requirements you can systematically tick off, but it's not that hard to know whether you are or not.

If you are a true Christian, the Holy Spirit dwells within you. And what is the sole purpose of the Holy Spirit?

> 'When the Advocate comes, whom I will send to you from the Father – the Spirit of truth who goes out from the Father – he will testify about me.' (John 15:26)

> 'But when he, the Spirit of truth, comes, he will guide you into all the truth. He will not speak on his own; he will speak only what he hears, and he will tell you what is yet to come. He will glorify me because it is from me that he will receive what he will make known to you. All that belongs to the Father is mine. That is why I said the Spirit will receive from me what he will make known to you.' (John 16:13-15)

It won't be hard to discover whether we are true Christians. The Holy Spirit will bring a fundamental change within you. There will now be a force within more persistent than your own thoughts and desires, that will steer you toward loyalty to Christ Jesus.

Your loyalty will no longer be for yourself, but for the Lord. Even if you do fail, there will now be a dissatisfaction within, and you will know you have wronged. The Holy Spirit will not let us live like unbelievers. He will not let us accept the pattern of this world as the standard we live by.

If you call yourself a Christian, but there is no desire within you that wants to love and obey the Lord Jesus Christ it is most likely, the Holy Spirit doesn't reside within. If you have doubts at this stage, go back to the Redemptive section of this book and make it right.

There is a good example in the New Testament of what happens when you become a Christian.

Saul of Tarsus was a zealous Pharisee who spat out murderous hatred toward Christians, because he believed with all his heart followers of Jesus were following a false doctrine.

But when he met Jesus on the road to Damascus, he repented and accepted Him as Lord and the Holy Spirit took up residence within Saul. Saul, whose name was changed to Paul, was now totally loyal to the Lord Jesus Christ.

The suffering Paul experienced for the sake of Christ was way beyond any human ability to handle. The power of God needed to be present in order for him to accomplish what he accomplished.[42]

Paul is now a willing bond-servant to Christ.

> If I must boast, I will boast of the things that show my weakness. (2 Corinthians 11:30)

> But he said to me, 'My grace is sufficient for you, for my power is made perfect in weakness.'
> Therefore I will boast all the more gladly about my weaknesses, so that Christ's power may rest on me. That is why, for Christ's sake, I delight in weaknesses, in insults, in hardships, in persecutions, in difficulties. For when I am weak, then I am strong. (2 Corinthians 12:9-10)

Paul is a good example of what happens when the Holy Spirit

---

42 2 Corinthians 11:23-30

comes within, he became totally loyal and obedient to the Lord Jesus. This is the standard we should be comparing ourselves with, not with someone in our church who is worse than us.

Obedience is the fruit that will want to be produced from deep within us, because of the Holy Spirit. It is up to us how much we want to allow this to happen.

Obedience should now be an integral part of our character if we acknowledge the Lord Jesus Christ. Making Jesus Lord, makes us subjects. All subjects must be obedient to their Lord.

If we are not being obedient, then Jesus Christ is simply not Lord.

Chapter 22

The Joy of Trials

One of the biggest lies leading people away from faith in Christ, is that Jesus promises we will live a successful, comfortable life and will be happy all the time because no trials will come our way. Or we may keep pushing forward for greater success in wealth, status, occupation, talents, giftings, promotions and other pursuits that make us important.

God does allow these, but for His glory, not ours.

Jesus tells us that trials and the testing of our faith will come, not to elevate us, but to humble us. This type of humbling does not bring us down, it elevates us because the light of Christ shines through, illuminating our lives, fulfilling us to overflowing.

While we are in our earthly bodies, trials will come. James goes further when he says we should be glad in our hearts when we are facing trials.

> Consider it pure joy, my brothers and sisters, whenever you face trials of many kinds, because you know that the testing of your faith produces perseverance. Let perseverance finish its work so that you may be mature and complete, not lacking anything. (James 1:2-4)

This statement sounds like an oxymoron.[43] Joy in suffering? How can you have joy when you are experiencing pain?

This is why we must understand Scripture and where it is coming from. Because if we don't, we become disillusioned and remain milk suckling babes or worse, let the seed of truth be snatched away or die.[44] Let us see why it is joyful when trials come.

Notice the joy referred to in Scripture is 'pure joy', which means it is from above. Human joy is fickle and vulnerable to our emotional state. Pure joy is from God, it is not swayed by circumstances. Whenever we are facing trials of any magnitude, big or small, we turn our face heavenward for His guidance.

> For it is God who works in you to will and to act in order to fulfil his good purpose. (Philippians 2:13)

When we are going through trials and acknowledge our weakness and die to ourselves, we call upon the Lord who gives us His strength to endure and persevere. Then you will know what pure joy is, because it is Christ who is surging through you.

Trials will come and they may not be what we expect. Or they may come because we don't get what we expect. Trials will come to test our faith, not so we may fail, but that we will grow.

This is where the joy comes in, because we know we are being transformed into the likeness of Christ Jesus. It is also to teach us that we can trust Him. Trials are to take our dependence off ourselves, others and other things, becoming more dependent on God.

When God led the Israelites out of Egypt, He deliberately led them to the desert. God needed to take away the ability for them

---

43 Oxymoron: a figure of speech in which apparently contradictory terms appear in conjunction

44 Mark 4:3-7

to rely on Egypt and themselves to live. He needed the Israelites to understand only He could fully sustain them.

He took away the necessities of life, food and water.

> When they came to Marah, they could not drink its water because it was bitter. So the people grumbled against Moses, saying, 'What are we to drink?' (Exodus 15:23-24)

> In the desert the whole community grumbled against Moses and Aaron. The Israelites said to them, 'If only we had died by the LORD's hand in Egypt. There we sat around pots of meat and ate all the food we wanted, but you have brought us out into this desert to starve this entire assembly to death.' (Exodus 16:2-3)

God knew He could sustain them, but they didn't. If they had got it, and taken their eyes off the visible and trusted the Invisible, they would have gone into the Promised Land much sooner. But because of their unbelief, they remained there another 40 years.

What has this wilderness experience of the Israelites got to do with us?

God gives us patterns. When God brought salvation to Israel by freeing them from slavery under Egypt, one of the first things He did was to test them. This is God's pattern. When we become Christians, God will test us. God needs us to understand that we can trust Him in all areas of our lives. God needed the Israelites to trust Him and He needs us to trust Him. It may not be as dramatic as the Israelites, but testing will come.

Another danger we can face is a trial of a different kind; not recognising God in the mundane. Discovering Christ in the everyday and the mundane is probably the greatest discovery affecting our relationship with Him.

When I first became a Christian, I was like an eager tiger, hungry to be used mightily by God. I was expecting exciting adventures and signs and wonders to go before me. I was caught up in the mindset that we are promised that we will be used mightily, and we will accomplish great exploits (which may or may not happen), but we can fall into a trap.

If we think Christianity is about us being used mightily or accomplishing much, then our eyes are in the wrong place.

If we are only finding God in the spectacular, we miss Him in the everyday and mundane. For most of us a large percentage of our lives is average and mundane. If we're not finding Christ in the so-called boring parts of our lives we are missing out on a huge portion that can be God-inclusive.

To discover Christ is the foundation carrying us further. When we become excited by God in the mundane, our faith is not dependent on the spectacular.

If this Christian life is deflating because nothing seems to be happening, discover Christ in the boring and you will discover the boring will become the spectacular. So, when the spectacular does happen, it is a natural extension of what we already have, which is a guard against pride.

Trials will come, albeit many shapes and forms, but we must recognise they are opportunities for us to grow and mature in Christ.

> Consider it pure joy, my brothers and sisters, whenever you face trials of many kinds… (James 1:2)

Chapter 23

Afflictions Appointed to Us

> That no man should be moved by these afflictions: for yourselves know that we are appointed thereunto. (KJV) ...so that no one would be unsettled by these trials. For you know quite well we are destined for them. (1 Thessalonians 3:3 NIV)

Now we have established that we will face trials for our benefit, we need to take a closer look at the nuts and bolts of afflictions and why they are important.

Afflictions will test our foundations.

> As for everyone who comes to me and hears my words and puts them into practice, I will show you what they are like. They are like a man building a house, who dug down deep and laid the foundation on rock. When a flood came, the torrent struck that house but could not shake it, because it was well built. (Luke 6:47-48)

When afflictions come, our foundation in Christ needs to be secure. We need to be meeting and walking obediently with Him. These foundations need to be established in Christ Jesus, which means we can't have a shallow relationship or a weak commitment.

To illustrate this more clearly look at some historical and geological facts about Nazareth.

Jesus grew up in the village of Nazareth. What made this town unique was where it is situated. It's nestled in the hills of Galilee and within these hills is an area like a bowl. Nazareth is located in this bowl made up of sand and fertile soil. Jesus, being a carpenter, knew what was required when building a house in this peculiar area. In the above parable concerning this, Jesus says of the strong house. 'They are like a man building a house, who dug down deep and laid the foundation on rock.' In Nazareth they needed to dig down deep before they hit the rock foundation.

There were obviously others who were not willing to go through that extra work and expense, so they laid their foundations in the sandy topsoil. For our foundations to be established in the Rock of Christ, we need to not only believe, but to obey.

Are we digging deep into Christ? Are we walking obediently before Him? If we're not practising these two fundamental requirements in times of normalcy, affliction can do great damage.

In the verses of Luke 6:47-48, Jesus uses two words, 'everyone' and 'when'. Everyone who follows Christ, will experience affliction. Our eyes need to be set on Christ, because He is the foundation keeping us safe. When affliction comes, we need to be hidden in Him, and responding the way the Holy Spirit wants us to respond.

If we're going to respond in the flesh, the Spirit will want us to die to that. If you respond in the Spirit, it will always be in line with God's will.

It may not be what we want, but God will work in us to act in order to fulfil His purpose.[45]

Afflictions come so the unnecessary parts of our lives can be stripped away.

---

45 Philippians 2:13

> 'I am the true vine, and my Father is the gardener. He cuts off every branch in me that bears no fruit, while every branch that does bear fruit he prunes so that it will be even more fruitful.' (John 15:1-2)

There are obvious things needing pruning; sins like pride, lust, sexual immorality, hypocrisy, lying and many more we should be aware of. But the not so obvious ones are what Christ wants to prune as well. Afflictions will come so what we think is important, but are in fact a hindrance, will be exposed and pruned. This latter pruning requires endurance and perseverance with Christ.

The harder to spot areas of our lives usually take a bit of time in the Refiner's fire, before the dross comes to the surface.

> 'For my thoughts are not your thoughts, neither are your ways my ways,' says the LORD.
> 'As the heavens are higher than the earth, so are my ways higher than your ways and my thoughts than your thoughts.' (Isaiah 55:8-9)

God's desire is for us to come in line with His way of thinking.

Afflictions come so we can learn to trust the Lord, no matter what.

> Who shall separate us from the love of Christ? Shall trouble or hardship or persecution or famine or nakedness or danger or sword? ...For I am convinced that neither death nor life, neither angels nor demons, neither the present nor the future, nor any powers, neither height nor depth, nor anything else in all creation, will be able to separate us from the love of God that is in Christ Jesus our Lord. (Romans 8:35, 38-39)

Whenever we go through a dark period, it's not a nice time, but if we remain true to God through it, we will understand with greater depth, we will remain spiritually intact through it. This is important, because when afflictions knock us around, we learn to trust our foundations will not give way.

In the darkness we remain in hope, because we know Christ is with us, and working for our good.

> And we know that in all things God works for the good of those who love him, who have been called according to his purpose. (Romans 8:28)

Chapter 24

Defeating the Giants

> And there we saw the giants, the sons of Anak, which come of the giants: and we were in our own sight as grasshoppers, and so we were in their sight. (Numbers 13:33 KJV)

This is about a sin that plagued me pre and post Christianity. When I became a Christian, this particular sin was not easy to dislodge, in fact, it was impossible, so it seemed.

This sin runs rife mainly amongst men, but women are not immune and it is usually kept secret. It does more damage than what we realise and is hard to dislodge. If you are a parent, the devil will use it as a back door to your family and keep you captive. One of the greatest sinful plagues that has nullified Christians and stripped them of their authority in Christ is sexual lust.

When I became a Christian, this sin would not let me go. For years I fought against it, but I was continually defeated. It was exactly how the Bible described it in Romans 7:19,

> For I do not do the good I want to do, but the evil I do not want to do – this I keep on doing.

During this time, my love for Christ never wavered, I never once wanted to turn my back on Him. This stronghold however was not going to let go. Even though I belonged to Christ, the damage of this sin was affecting me spiritually.

It was more than this sin trying to take me out. It was my willingness that allowed it.

> When tempted, no one should say, 'God is tempting me.' For God cannot be tempted by evil, nor does he tempt anyone; but each person is tempted when they are dragged away by their own evil desire and enticed. (James 1:13-14)

I allowed these evil desires to live, I allowed this fleshly desire to survive.

No matter how determined I was, this particular sin would not be beaten. Christ showed me a simple way to overcome it.

> But let all who take refuge in you be glad; let them ever sing for joy. Spread your protection over them, that those who love your name may rejoice in you. The LORD is a refuge for the oppressed, a stronghold in times of trouble. The LORD is my rock, my fortress and my deliverer; my God is my rock, in whom I take refuge, my shield and the horn of my salvation, my stronghold. (Psalm 5:11, 9:9, 18:2)

This is what Christ taught me, simply choose to surrender to Him. And this was the amazing thing, when I surrendered to Christ, there was no fight. Before I would either just give in to it, or resist it (usually in my own strength), but it would hang around, like someone knocking insistently on your back door. But every time I submitted to Christ, this temptation would disappear. I need to be clear here. When I submit to Christ, it needs to be full submission, not a casual, half-hearted submission. I die to self and become hidden in Christ, I go into His Presence and wholeheartedly, dwell in His safety. I choose to operate in the Spirit and not the flesh.

> The mind governed by the flesh is death, but the mind governed by the Spirit is life and peace. (Romans 8:6)

> Then Jesus said to his disciples, 'Whoever wants to be my disciple must deny themselves and take up their cross and follow me. For whoever wants to save their life will lose it, but whoever loses their life for me will find it.' (Matthew 16:24-25)

Here is another powerful truth, it's not us making this happen. It's the Holy Spirit drawing us into this realm of safety, we simply have to choose who we are going to obey.

The difficulty for me was not the temptation, but the decision to either submit to the flesh or the Spirit. This becomes the pivotal moment. John 15:4-5 becomes much more meaningful,

> Remain in me, as I also remain in you. No branch can bear fruit by itself, it must remain in the vine. Neither can you bear fruit unless you remain in me. I am the vine; you are the branches. If you remain in me and I in you, you will bear much fruit; apart from me you can do nothing.

For me, sexual lust was a giant in my life that would not free me, but when I hide myself in Christ, Christ is the Giant to giants. This lust giant loses his hold over me.

I must go deeper now into my personal challenge. For most people, surrendering to Christ would be sufficient to keep this sin at bay, but for me, it was subtly different. Even though it was absolutely true that I experienced real victory over this sin through

Christ Jesus, there was something much deeper needing to be dealt with.

Even though I had the ability to choose not to give into this sin, the attraction of it was still dangerously powerful. For many years this remained the case, I thought it was something I had to continually contend with. I didn't realise this sin had not been completely dislodged.

> To fear the Lord is to hate evil; I hate pride and arrogance, evil behaviour and perverse speech. (Proverbs 8:13)

Even though I didn't want this sin, I didn't hate it. There was a part of me that still loved it. Therefore, the root of that sin was still able to remain buried in my soul. Even though the manifestation or the results of this sin were eradicated and cut away, there remained the root waiting for the time to strike.

> When tempted, no one should say, 'God is tempting me.' For God cannot be tempted by evil, nor does he tempt anyone; but each person is tempted when they are dragged away by their own evil desire and enticed. (James 1:13-14)

It was this evil which remained as a root within me needing to be dislodged and ripped out of my life.

One startling truth about the effects of this root, is that it affected more than me. It affected my wife causing agitation in her spirit, which I was blind to.

It was through my wife this root was finally dealt with properly. God was able to use her to fish out this root which had successfully hidden itself. As painful (for both of us) as this process was, it made me finally confront this sin and truly repent of it. It was only when I came before God totally naked (figuratively) and experienced a real hatred for this sin, the process of ripping this root out started in earnest. Repentance, transparency and confession were the processes God took me through, not only with my wife, but with a Christian couple we are accountable to.

This giant affected my life, even when I became a Christian. And even when I thought it was dealt with, God knew there needed to be more surgery.

Even though the process may be long, the desire of God is always this:

'So if the Son sets you free, you will be free indeed.' (John 8:36)

It has been over a year since that repentance, and I can honestly testify that sin has no magnetic attraction for me. God has faithfully rooted it out, but I still depend on His refuge. I ask Him daily to keep me free and He is more than willing to protect.

Part 5

God's Will for Us

Chapter 25

Numbers 1 – Conscripted

What a perfect way to start this particular subject concerning God's call on our lives.

The first thing mentioned in Numbers is conscription.

> Take a census of the whole Israelite community by their clans and families, listing every man by name, one by one. You and Aaron are to count according to their divisions all the men in Israel who are twenty years old or more and able to serve in the army. (Numbers 1:2-3)

From the start of our Christian journey we're conscripted into God's army. We are now active members participating in this spiritual army and it's no small thing. We're in spiritual warfare.

> The weapons we fight with are not the weapons of the world. On the contrary, they have divine power to demolish strongholds. We demolish arguments and every pretension that sets itself up against the knowledge of God, and we take captive every thought to make it obedient to Christ. And we will be ready to punish every act of disobedience, once your obedience is complete. (2 Corinthians 10:4-6)

From the start we are on active duty. Whether we are on the front line or far from the front line, the battle we face does not go away. Even if we are not doing some great exploit for the Lord, we are important members of His army, no matter where God has placed us.

An active soldier is alert and focused and not distracted.

> No one serving as a soldier gets entangled in civilian affairs, but rather tries to please his commanding officer. (2 Timothy 2:4)

No matter where we find ourselves, we are to remain faithful and focused on Christ, our Commander and Chief.

The Bible makes it very clear, how we are involved in spiritual warfare.

> For we wrestle not against flesh and blood, but against principalities, against powers, against the rulers of the darkness of this world, against spiritual wickedness in high places. Wherefore take unto you the whole armour of God, that ye may be able to withstand in the evil day, and having done all, to stand. Stand therefore, having your loins girt about with truth, and having on the breastplate of righteousness; And your feet shod with the preparation of the gospel of peace; Above all, taking the shield of faith, wherewith ye shall be able to quench all the fiery darts of the wicked. And take the helmet of salvation, and the sword of the Spirit, which is the word of God. (Ephesians 6:12-17 KJV)

The difference about this armour is that you don't take it off. We're to be maturing in knowledge and action, in all these key areas.

No Christian is useless, all are conscripted by God. When we side with Christ, we automatically have an enemy in the realm of the spirit and the flesh. Our spiritual enemies will never leave us alone, they will always try to distract us from Christ, while trying not to be noticed.

Our carnal nature battles against this relationship as well, we must be putting it to death daily.

Whether we are battling at a personal level, or something outside ourselves, we will always be active members of God's army.

Whenever we surrender to Christ and are abiding in the True Vine we're participating in spiritual warfare. It could be anything, if Christ is involved, you are on active duty. Many of our Christian activities do not seem very war-like, but whatever they are, the devil will not be impressed.

Satan's goal is to remove this world and the universe from the Lord Jesus Christ.

> How you have fallen from heaven, morning star, son of the dawn! You have been cast down to the earth, you who once laid low the nations! You said in your heart, 'I will ascend to the heavens, I will raise my throne above the stars of God; I will sit enthroned on the mount of assembly, on the utmost heights of Mount *of the north*. I will ascend above the tops of the clouds, I will make myself like the Most High.' But you are brought down to the realm of the dead, to the depths of the pit. (Isaiah 14:12-15)

Satan believes he can still accomplish this and will until he is thrown into the pit of hell by Christ. Until then there is a war raging and we as Christians are part of that battle.

Chapter 26

Numbers 2-4 – Priestly Duties

The second chapter of Numbers records the placement of tribes around the Tabernacle.

Note the distance between the tribes and the Tabernacle and what role the Levites had in this.

> The Israelites are to camp around the tent of meeting some distance from it, each of them under their standard and holding the banner of their family. (Numbers 2:2)

All the tribes were strategically placed around the Tabernacle at a distance because the Levites were to camp between the tribes and the Tabernacle.

The Levites were the priestly tribe of Israel. They were the only tribe who could minister in the Tabernacle and they were the only tribe who could handle the sacred objects and fittings of the Tent of Meeting.

Chapters 3 and 4 go into more detail about the Levites. There were four family lines within the Levites, and they had specific duties to perform. God warned them not to overstep their responsibilities or severe punishment would result.

The Kohathites are a good example.

> See that the Kohathite tribal clans are not destroyed from among the Levites. So that they may live and not die when they come near the most holy things, do this for them: Aaron and his sons are to go into the sanctuary and assign to each man his work and what he is to carry. But the Kohathites must not go in to look at the holy things, even for a moment, or they will die. (Numbers 4:18-20)

We will look at the significance of this a little later.
What was the duty of the Levites?

> Bring the tribe of Levi and present them to Aaron the priest to assist him. They are to perform duties for him and for the whole community at the tent of meeting by doing the work of the tabernacle. They are to take care of all the furnishings of the tent of meeting, fulfilling the obligations of the Israelites by doing the work of the tabernacle. (Numbers 3:6-8)

The significance of this is neglected in our lives.

> The Israelites are to camp around the tent of meeting some distance from it... (Numbers 2:2)

The tribes of Israel were to camp at a distance from the Tabernacle because the Levites were to camp in between them.
This is significant for us as Christians and if we are not getting this right we are in danger of getting our other duties wrong.
When we become Christians, we become priests of the Most High God.

> ...and from Jesus Christ, who is the faithful witness, the firstborn from the dead, and the ruler of the kings of the earth.

Numbers 2-4 – Priestly Duties

> To him who loves us and has freed us from our sins by his blood, and has made us to be a kingdom and priests to serve his God and Father – to him be glory and power for ever and ever! Amen. (Revelation 1:5-6)

Our priestly duties will always be more important strategically to God than any other duties we may carry out. The placement of the Levites (priests) was between the Tabernacle and other tribes. It was always the priests making it possible for the other tribes to come into the Tabernacle.

Ministering to the Lord will always take priority over what we do for God. No matter what we are doing, we must always be in communication with Christ. It is so easy to become too busy.

God has made it clear in His Word we must protect our time with Him and this truth is found throughout the Bible, especially the Gospel. The great men and women of faith that accomplished great things for the Lord always made their priestly calling priority over their specific calling.

If we get this wrong, we will fall into the trap of operating in our own strength, wisdom or understanding. When we are making our priestly calling a priority, we need not worry about what God wants us to do, because He will make it clear to us and make the way possible. Wherever we are placed, our priestly duty will always remain important.

Numbers chapter 3 goes into more detail about the specific duties of the Levites.

> Give the Levites to Aaron and his sons; they are the Israelites who are to be given wholly to him. Appoint Aaron and his sons to serve as priests; anyone else who approaches the sanctuary is to be put to death. (Numbers 3:9-10)

God made it clear no one could approach the Tabernacle unless they were first appointed. Only those appointed to handling the sacred utensils and objects of the Tabernacle were permitted, or they would die. This was so, because they were coming into the very presence of God.

If we believe we are doing what God has called us to do we have been put in a position where we are handling the sacred things of God. Whenever Christ chooses to work through you, these are sacred things of God. Do we respect and understand the position we hold?

The Levites were appointed by God, we too must be appointed by God.

In almost all of his epistles Paul writes at the beginning of his letters, how he and fellow servants were servants of Christ by the will of God and not by man.[46] Just as the Levites were appointed by God to carry out His sacred duties which no other tribe were permitted, we too are set aside by God to carry out His sacred purpose.

If we're not maintaining our priestly duty and continually seeking the Lord we are in danger of operating in our own strength.

If we are operating in our own strength, the next scenario becomes alarming. If we are doing what we believe God has called us to do, but we are not faithful in our priestly duties, what we think are the sacred things of God either lack His authority or worse still, become counterfeit things.

What we are bringing before the Lord or doing in the name of the Lord, Christ may not be able to anoint it, or they simply become man-made. It may have the appearance of holiness, but, are in danger of being empty vessels. They look holy, but in fact, are dead objects.

---

46 Romans 1:1, 1 Corinthians 1:1, 2 Corinthians 1:1, Galatians 1:1, Ephesians 1:1, Philippians 1:1, Colossians 1:1, 1 Timothy 1:1, 2 Timothy 1:1, Titus 1:1, Philemon 1:1

Another sign we are not consistently performing our priestly duties is experiencing continual defeat in our personal lives. Seeking the Lord instils His strength, therefore we have a greater ability for victory rather than defeat.

> The LORD Is my rock, my fortress and my deliverer; my God is my rock, in whom I take refuge, my shield and the horn of my salvation, my stronghold. (Psalm 18:2)

> But whatever were gains to me I now consider loss for the sake of Christ. What is more, I consider everything a loss because of the surpassing worth of knowing Christ Jesus my Lord, for whose sake I have lost all things. I consider them garbage that I may gain Christ and be found in him, not having a righteousness of my own that comes from the law, but that which is through faith in Christ – the righteousness that comes from God on the basis of faith. (Philippians 3:7-9)

When we're consistently coming into the Presence of Christ and obeying His teachings, our foundations become planted in the Rock of Christ. When the storms come, we will stand. Being priests gives us the ability to connect with God on an intimate personal level. But neglecting this is dangerous.

The danger of neglecting our priestly duties while carrying out the duties of God, is that you can still carry out the duties of God. That's why many Christians (or so-called Christians) can still operate in leadership while still blatantly sinning. It is something we need to take seriously, because sin will blind us and we are capable of deceiving ourselves.

Numbers 2-4 reminds us of the importance God placed on the Levites who were given the responsibility of ministering and performing His duties. Through Jesus Christ, we have all become priests.

We have been given the right to come into Tabernacle of the Holy God. But we can only enter through the leading of the Spirit and not the flesh.

If we are faithful to this call, Christ will equip us with His power and authority to accomplish all our earthly duties. The priestly call is required of every Christian, we must diligently maintain it.

Chapter 27

Numbers 2 – Placement

Numbers chapter two deals with where the tribes of Israel are to be placed. A census of all the men over the age of twenty in those tribes was taken.

As the first chapter of this section says, all Christians are conscripted into God's army. It doesn't matter where God places us, we will always be active members of God's army.

In the second chapter, God takes a census for determining who belongs to what tribe. And these tribes were strategically placed around the Tabernacle. The placement of the tribes represents the placement of Christians today.

One of the biggest concerns among Christians is, 'What is God's will for our lives?' It can become an obsession or feel like you are only on the side-line watching. Through the picture of the tribes of Israel being placed around the Tabernacle, God reveals how we are more than likely, where He wants us. To be accomplishing the will of Christ becomes quite simple.

It's no accident what we do for God is the last of His priorities. Once you understand what God's priorities are and put them into practice, you can truly fulfil His will, whatever that may be.

If we are taking God's way to success seriously, what we are to do for Him will take care of itself.

The placing of the tribes around the Tabernacle is a good lesson for us to learn.

When the Israelites were in the desert they moved from place to place.

> On the day the tabernacle, the tent of the covenant law, was set up, the cloud covered it. From evening till morning the cloud above the tabernacle looked like fire. Whenever the cloud lifted from above the tent, the Israelites set out; wherever the cloud settled, the Israelites encamped. At the LORD's command the Israelites set out, and at his command they encamped. As long as the cloud stayed over the tabernacle, they remained in camp. (Numbers 9:15-18)

Whenever the tribes moved, they resettled in the same order.

Wherever they went, the placing of the tribes remained the same. This is important because the tribes were always placed around the Tabernacle. The Tent of Meeting always remained central. No matter where God moved them.

As Christians, it doesn't matter where God has placed us, Christ must always remain the central focus of our lives. Whether we are at an oasis or in a dry barren desert, Christ must remain our central focus.

Whether we are on the front line or vanguard, Christ must remain our central focus.

If we are not where God wants us to be, He will make us aware where we should be. But be aware, sometimes we may feel that where we are, is not a place of productivity. It may however be exactly where God wants you.

I can personally testify to this.

When God placed me in a processing factory, I reminded God this was not my calling. My refusal to accept this is where God wanted me lasted for two years. Only when I died to my will, and accepted His will, did things start to change. Many encounters with God, and illuminations of His Word happened at my workplace.

What I thought was a barren desert became a great oasis.

The important factor is, God knows what He is doing in our lives, we are simply to trust Him and be obedient to wherever He has called us.

It is not what we are doing that determines how successful we are, but how Christ remains central to wherever we are that makes us successful.

You may feel you are in a place of barrenness, but Christ is still central. You are more successful in God's eyes than someone blazing a trail in the name of Christ when Christ is not central for them.

God has called us and has good works in store for us to do, but these works on their own merit, won't make us successful.

It is the transforming power of Christ we allow into our lives that determines how successful we are.

Chapter 28

Knowing the Good, Pleasing and Perfect Will of God

God desires for all of us to live a successful life. This book has not promised that you will be destined for greatness, or become a mighty instrument in God's hand, leaving your mark in this world. You may indeed accomplish great things on this earth and be a mighty instrument of God that brings noticeable changes in this world. But these things are not the sum of success.

The Apostle Paul sums it up perfectly:

> What is more, I consider everything a loss because of the surpassing worth of knowing Christ Jesus my Lord, for whose sake I have lost all things. I consider them garbage, that I may gain Christ. (Philippians 3:8)

Paul's greatest success was to know Christ, yet he was used mightily by God to establish His church. Paul fully understood where his success came from, therefore the works he did for Christ, carried God's authority.

Once we understand God's way to success, the will He has for our lives will naturally fall into place. If we live a life where Christ is always central, whether we affect millions of lives worldwide or spend our lives interceding in the hidden closet, success is guaranteed.

Success is not what we can accomplish on this earth, but how much of our lives is surrendered to the Father, Son and the Holy Spirit. Everything we do on this earth has to flow from this. This means that the heart of Christ will be manifesting itself through you. Whether it be evangelising, serving, interceding, shepherding, helping, encouraging, edifying, teaching, prophesying, being a light on the hill and much more.

Wherever you find yourself and whatever you are doing, may you do it unto the Lord.

> Whatever you do, work at it with all your heart, as working for the Lord, not for human masters, since you know that you will receive an inheritance from the Lord as a reward. It is the Lord Christ you are serving. (Colossians 3:23-24)

And the reason why we do this, is because we live in a world that is under the influence of the Tree of Knowledge, and we are not.

> Therefore, my dear friends, as you have always obeyed – not only in my presence, but now much more in my absence – continue to work out your salvation with fear and trembling, for it is God who works in you to will and to act in order to fulfil his good purpose. Do everything without grumbling or arguing, so that you may become blameless and pure, 'children of God without fault in a warped and crooked generation. Then you will shine among them like stars in the sky.' (Philippians 2:12-15)

True success can only be found in the Triune God (Father, Son and the Holy Spirit). This is true because before anything was created, God existed. There was perfect unity and nothing outside of this could add to the completeness. They lacked nothing and nothing could be added to their perfection.

'I and the Father are one.' (John 10:30)

The Son is the radiance of God's glory and the exact representation of his being... (Hebrews 1:3)

...and the Holy Spirit descended on him in bodily form like a dove. And a voice came from heaven: 'You are my Son, whom I love; with you I am well pleased.' (Luke 3:22)

'All that belongs to the Father is mine. That is why I said the Spirit will receive from me what he will make known to you.' (John 16:15)

Why is this important and relevant to us?

Because the sole reason we even exist, is so we may share in this. We just have a glimpse of it now, but when we go on to heavenly glory, it will become an absolute reality for us.

God's way to success is not based on the pattern of this world, but based on a Person, the Lord Jesus Christ and everything He accomplishes.

Conclusion

Hopefully by now, success doesn't mean the greatness of you or me, but the greatness of God (Father, Son and the Holy Spirit). Purpose-filled lives do not come from purpose-driven activities, but from the One who gives us purpose.

We have the capacity to be successful on our own, and many millions accomplish this, but what does it accomplish in the eternal scale of things. We can fill our lives with activities and accomplishments, but do these things truly fulfil us? We can even accomplish much in the name of Jesus, without Him being involved.

True success can only be accomplished when the foundations are established in the Lord Jesus Christ. Everything we do and accomplish outside of Christ, is a house built on sand and the end of that house is never good.

Only God knows what it takes for us to be successful and He has not left us searching in the dark trying to find it. He has given us His Word which is both Scripture and Jesus Christ.

> In the beginning was the Word, and the Word was with God, and the Word was God. (John 1:1)

> All Scripture is God-breathed and is useful for teaching, rebuking, correcting and training in righteousness, so that the servant of God may be thoroughly equipped for every good work. (2 Timothy 3:16-17)

God's Way to Success

No matter where we find ourselves or what we are doing, we'll always be successful if we follow God's way to success.

*Thanks for reading this book.
If you would like to get in contact,
please email:*
jason.selinagroube@outlook.com

www.ingramcontent.com/pod-product-compliance
Lightning Source LLC
Chambersburg PA
CBHW051433290426
44109CB00016B/1537